Ready for First Certificate

Workbook

Roy Norris

MACMILLAN

Macmillan Education
Between Towns Road, Oxford OX4 3PP
A division of Macmillan Publishers Limited
Companies and representatives throughout the world

ISBN 0 333 928253

First published 2001

Designed by DP Press Ltd, Sevenoaks
Illustrated by DP Press Ltd.
Cover idea by Xen Media Ltd.

Author's acknowledgements
I would particularly like to thank my editor, Sarah Ashton, for her hard work and dedication, and my wife, Azucena, for all her help and support.

The author and publishers would like to thank Polly Clark and Malcolm Wren.

The author and publishers would like to thank the following for permission to reproduce their material:
Caledonian Discovery Ltd for extracts from *Winter Activities* brochure on the internet www.lochaber.co.uk/fingal/winter.htm; News International Syndication, for extracts and adaptations from 'The car they will deliver by fax' by Jerome Burne, from *The Sunday Times* 12 March 2000, copyright © Times Newspapers Limited, London; 'With a knife he'll survive anywhere' by Mark Chadbourn from *Times Weekend* 22 January 2000, copyright © Mark Chadbourn/Times Newspapers Limited, London; 'Dyslexic teenager turns into top entrepreneur' by Claire Oldfield from *The Sunday Times* 28 November 1999, copyright © Times Newspapers Limited, London; 'The Little School of Calm' by Anna Selby from *Times Magazine* 5 September 1998, copyright © Times Newspapers Limited; 'Meals on Wheels' by Sheila Keating from *Times Magazine* 12 September 1998, copyright © Times Newspapers Limited; Woman's Realm, for 'Where did you get that dress?' by Sally Brickway, *Woman's Realm* 26 October 1999; Woman's Weekly, for 'Even if I was down on my knees I couldn't give up on my animals' by Ktima Heathcote in *Woman's Weekly* 24 August 1999.

The author and publishers would like to thank the following for permission to reproduce their photographs:
Art Directors and Trip p75; BBC Photographic Library p82; Camera press p110; Corbis pp67, Corbis/Sean Aidan 7, Corbis/David Allen 26 (tr), Corbis/Bettmann 3, Corbis/Bettmann 23 (ml), Corbis/Mitchell Gerber 2, Corbis/Mitchell Gerber 26 (tm), Corbis/Mitchell Greber 31, Corbis/Joel Rogers 7; Haddon Davis © MHELT p23 (bl); Image Bank pp115, 121; Dorling Kindersley Picture Library p106 (tl, tm, tr); Oxford and County Newspapers p42; PA Photos pp59, PA Photos/Phil Nobel 95; Stone pp35, 90, 101, 115.

Printed and bound in Spain by Mateu Cromo SA Madrid

2005 2004
10 9 8 7 6 5 4

Contents

1 Lifestyle

Reading

FCE Part 3 **Gapped text**

1 You are going to read a magazine article about a woman who buys clothes from famous people and then sells them in her shop. Complete the following table as you read the article.

Name of Star	Former possessions
Cher	*shoes, jewellery, furniture*

WHERE DID YOU GET THAT DRESS?

As a young child Gwen Crowley would often borrow her older sister's clothes and dress up as a princess or an actress. Gwen, 38, still likes to put on other people's clothes, only now the blouses and dresses she wears used to belong to famous film stars. She also buys clothes from celebrities such as Cher in order to sell them in her second-hand clothes shop, Star Wares, in Los Angeles.

Cher tends to get rid of a lot of her things each year and we just go over with a truck and pick them up. I've met her a few times, although **I've never been wearing any of her clothes at the time.** 0 I

I love Cher's style. I have her shoes, her jewellery and even some of her furniture. They're a real bargain because I pay less for them than she did originally. **Many of my customers don't wear the clothes they buy** and just keep them as memorabilia. 1

I also had a denim shirt which I bought from Mel Gibson. I wore it all the time, **even when I was decorating the house.** 2 I really liked that shirt and it was great fun telling people which famous person owned it before.

My first ever purchase was a white T-shirt of Cher's that had peace signs all over it and which I wore until it fell to pieces. But my favourite item of clothing at the moment is a black shirt of hers by Ghost. I'm a little bigger than her, so **her clothes are often quite tight on me.** 3 It's a plain, flowing shirt that feels really nice to wear – **except when it's raining.**

4 The shirt shrank and the sleeves, which were long, suddenly went up past my elbows. I was really upset. I had to go into the bathroom and put it under the dryer. Luckily it survived. Now I wear it just about everywhere – around the house, out shopping, at work.

Sometimes I see Cher in magazines and think, I'd like that top or dress, and a few months later it comes into the shop. If she's worn the item on a CD cover or something, I don't usually buy it because then it becomes a collector's item and **can be very expensive.** 5

Although my husband doesn't share my passion, he was delighted when I bought him **Cary Grant's silver cigarette case** for his 40th birthday. 6 It's a real talking point at parties because my husband is called Lou and everybody asks: 'Why does it say Cary?' When he tells them, they're amazed.

It's wonderful to have a part of someone that you admire, that you can actually hold, look at, enjoy and wear. At the moment I've got my eye on **a very special costume from my all time favourite TV programme.** 7 It's not the sort of thing you can wear to the shops, but it would certainly attract attention at a fancy dress party!

2 Read the following instructions for this Part 3 Reading task.

Eight sentences have been removed from the article. Choose from the sentences **A–I** the one which fits each space (**1–7**). There is one extra sentence which you do not need to use. There is an example at the beginning **(0)**.

How to go about it

- Be careful with the pronouns *it* and *they* in the sentences below. In each case they refer to something different. When you make your choice, check carefully that *the whole sentence* fits in with the meaning of the text before and after the space.
- To help you do this parts of the text above are written in **bold**. Use these clues to match each sentence to the correct space.

A If it was something I really liked, though, I would buy it, no matter how much it cost.
B I got paint on it and all sorts of other stains, but it broke my heart when I finally had to throw it away.
C It's in a cloth bag and has the actor's name inscribed on the front.
D However, I like to enjoy my clothes and I always wear Cher's things until they're worn out.
E It's Dr McCoy's original tunic from the *Star Trek* series.
F I once wore it to a TV interview and got caught in a storm.
G They don't go with any of my other clothes but they still look good on me!
H This one, though, is a lot looser and fits me perfectly.
I I'm not sure how she'd react if she saw me in one of her old sweaters or skirts.

3 For each of the following definitions find a word in the text. The numbers in brackets refer to the boxed numbers in the text. The word you need is in the same paragraph.

1. famous people (eg film stars) (introduction) ______________ (n)
2. collect; go and get (phrasal verb) (0) ______________ (v)
3. something which is good value and cheaper than normal (1) ______________ (n)
4. things you collect because they are connected with a person or event (1) ______________ (n)
5. something you have bought (3) ______________ (n)
6. became smaller (4) ______________ (v)
7. extremely pleased (6) ______________ (adj)
8. a costume you wear in order to look like a well-known person or thing (2 words) (7) ______________ (n)

4 In each of the sentences below, complete the spaces to form a phrase which has the same meaning as the words in brackets. Each of the phrases is in the text.

1. I'm going to dress ________ ________ *Batman* for Jackie's fancy dress party. (put on clothes to look like)
2. My jeans were so old they eventually fell ________ ________ . (broke up into different parts)
3. I've got ________ ________ ________ a beautiful cottage that I saw for sale recently. (am interested in having)
4. It broke ________ ________ when I finally had to throw away my old jumper. (made me sad)

Vocabulary

Wordlist on page 202 of the Coursebook

A Clothes

1 Use the clues below to help you complete the grid. When you have all the answers you will find an extra item of vocabulary for number 12 down.

1 an adjective to describe clothes which look old and worn
2 a piece of cloth worn round the neck to keep you warm
3 loose top and trousers, worn by people during exercise or when training for sport
4 an adjective describing clothes which keep you dry
5 a shirt for girls or women
6 clothes which are simple and not colourful
7 a type of hat worn by motorcyclists and soldiers for protection
8 a narrow piece of leather or cloth worn round the waist
9 a piece of jewellery which you wear round your wrist
10 a type of jacket, often part of school uniform
11 soft shoes worn in the house

2 Use one of the adjectives from the Wordlist on page 202 of the Coursebook to describe each of the following items of clothing. The first one has been done for you **(0)**.

0

a shabby overcoat

1
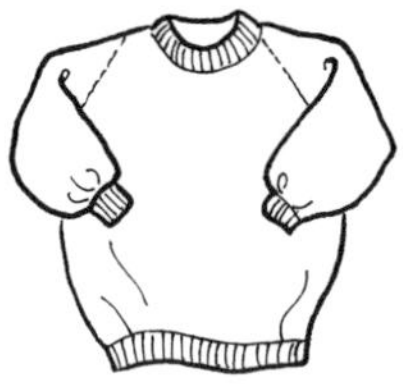

2
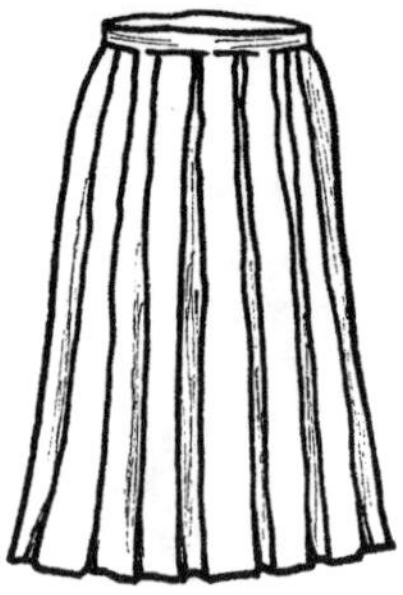

3
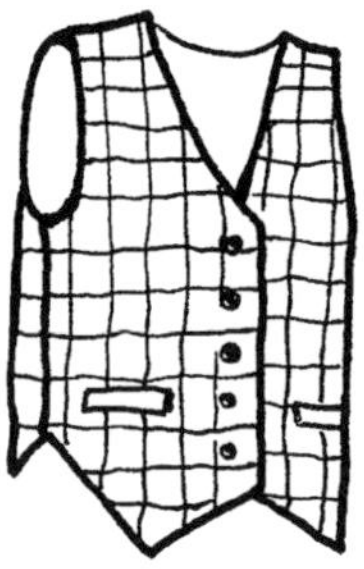

4

5

6

7

B *Get*

Lexical phrase list on page 124 and Phrasal verb list on page 122

1 Complete each of the spaces with one of the words in the box to form a verb with *get*. The resulting verb with *get* should have the same meaning as the verb in brackets. The first one has been done for you (0).

on	off	over	away	~~to~~	out of	back	by

0 We didn't get ___*to*___ (arrive in) London until midnight.
1 I don't earn very much but I get __________ (manage to live) OK.
2 It took him a long time to get __________ (recover from) the flu.
3 What time do you think you'll get __________ (return)?
4 He was shot while trying to get __________ (escape) from the police.
5 He doesn't get __________ (have a good relationship) with his sister.
6 You have to get __________ (leave) the bus at the shopping centre.
7 I can't seem to get __________ (stop) the habit of biting my nails.

2 Complete each of the spaces with an appropriate word from the box.

rid	touch	ready	worse	paid	dressed	trouble	mark

1 I haven't written to Steve for ages – I really ought to get in __________ with him.
2 When he was 14 he got into __________ with the police.
3 I think footballers get __________ far too much.
4 The car kept breaking down so we decided to get __________ of it.
5 I spent the day getting __________ for Christmas, buying presents and cooking.
6 What __________ did you get for your writing homework?
7 My throat's getting __________ . I think I ought to see a doctor.
8 Why are you still in your pyjamas. Hurry up and get __________ !

C Word combinations

1 Both the words in each of the pairs below can be used in combination with one of the words in the box. Write an appropriate noun from the box in each of the spaces. There is an example at the beginning **(0)**.

event	premiere	party	~~jacket~~	story	interview	agency	industry

0 dinner sports	*jacket*	**4** television job	__________
1 fashion film	__________	**5** social sporting	__________
2 model news	__________	**6** film world	__________
3 political birthday	__________	**7** news bedtime	__________

2 Study the word combinations in exercise 1 for one minute. Then look at the words in the box and cover the exercise. How many combinations can you remember?

Language focus

Grammar reference on page 206 of the Coursebook

A Adverbs of frequency

For each of the following sentences decide if the position of the adverb of frequency is correct. If it is not correct, rewrite the sentence.

1 As a young child Gwen Crowley would <u>often</u> borrow her older sister's clothes.

____

2 I've met her a few times, although I <u>never</u> have been wearing any of her clothes at the time.

____

3 Her clothes <u>often</u> are quite tight on me.

____

4 I see <u>sometimes</u> Cher in magazines.

____

5 If she's worn the item on a CD cover, I don't <u>usually</u> buy it.

____

B *Used to* and *would*

In the following extract from the reading text, decide whether the underlined verbs can be used with:

a both *used to* and *would*
b only *used to*
c neither *used to* nor *would*

I also **(1)** <u>had</u> a denim shirt which I **(2)** <u>bought</u> from Mel Gibson. I **(3)** <u>wore</u> it all the time, even when I was decorating. I really **(4)** <u>liked</u> that shirt and it was great fun telling people which famous actor **(5)** <u>owned</u> it before.

1 ____________
2 ____________
3 ____________
4 ____________
5 ____________

Use of English

FCE Part 3

Transformations

Complete the second sentence so that it has a similar meaning to the first sentence, using the word given. **Do not change the word given**. You must use between two and five words, including the word given. There is an example at the beginning **(0)**.

0 She often went abroad on holiday before she got married.
would
She *would often go* ____________ abroad on holiday before she got married.

1 We tend not to eat much at lunchtime.
usually
We ______________________________ at lunchtime.

2 I almost always go out on Saturday night.
ever
I ______________________________ at home on Saturday night.

3 The stadium was always full on the day of the cup final.
used
The stadium ______________________________ full on the day of the cup final.

4 He phones me at work all the time, and I've told him not to.
keeps
He ________________________________ at work and I've told him not to.

5 Anna rarely gets less than 70% in her English exam.
rare
It ________________________________ get less than 70% in her English exam.

6 I can't wait to go on holiday.
forward
I'm really ________________________________ on holiday.

7 We've been back at school for two weeks and I still find it hard to get up early.
used
We've been back at school for two weeks and I'm still
________________________________ up early.

FCE Part 1

Multiple choice cloze

Read the text below and decide which answer **A**, **B**, **C** or **D** best fits each space. There is an example at the beginning **(0)**.

A life with birds

For nearly 17 years David Cope has worked **(0)** _as_ one of the Tower of London's Yeoman Warders, **(1)** ________ known to tourists as Beefeaters. David, 64, lives in a three-bedroomed flat right at the **(2)** ________ of the Byward Tower, one of the gatehouses. '**(3)** ________ our bedroom we have a marvellous view of Tower Bridge and the Thames.' says David.

The Tower of London is famous **(4)** ________ its ravens, the large black birds which have lived there for over three centuries. David was immediately fascinated by the birds and when he was **(5)** ________ the post of Raven Master eight years ago he had no **(6)** ________ in accepting it. 'The birds have now become my life and I'm always **(7)** ________ of the fact that I am **(8)** ________ a tradition. The legend says that if the ravens leave the Tower, England will fall to enemies, and it's my job to **(9)** ______ sure this doesn't happen!'

David **(10)** ________ about four hours a day to the care of the ravens. He has grown to love them and the **(11)** ________ that he lives right next to them is ideal. 'I can **(12)** ________ a close eye on them all the time, and not just when I'm working.'

(13) ________ , David's wife Mo was not **(14)** ________ on the idea of life in the Tower, but she too will be sad to leave when he retires next year. 'When we look out of our windows we see history **(15)** ________ around us, and we are taking it in and storing it up for our future memories.'

0	**A** like	**B** _as_	**C** because	**D** at
1	**A** more	**B** better	**C** sooner	**D** very
2	**A** height	**B** summit	**C** peak	**D** top
3	**A** Since	**B** Out	**C** From	**D** Through
4	**A** for	**B** because	**C** of	**D** by
5	**A** award	**B** applied	**C** presented	**D** offered
6	**A** regret	**B** delay	**C** hesitation	**D** choice
7	**A** aware	**B** knowing	**C** pleased	**D** delighted
8	**A** holding	**B** maintaining	**C** surviving	**D** lasting
9	**A** take	**B** make	**C** have	**D** keep
10	**A** devotes	**B** spends	**C** passes	**D** provides
11	**A** reason	**B** chance	**C** opportunity	**D** fact
12	**A** hold	**B** have	**C** keep	**D** put
13	**A** Firstly	**B** First of all	**C** At first	**D** First
14	**A** interested	**B** keen	**C** fond	**D** happy
15	**A** every	**B** all	**C** much	**D** so

Writing

Letters

In the Writing Paper of the FCE exam you will have to write a letter. Some of the reasons for which we write letters are given in the table below.

1 Look at each of the sentences **1–10** and decide if the English used is formal or informal. Then put the number for each sentence in the correct column of the table below, next to the appropriate reason for writing. The first one has been done for you.

	Formal	Informal
Complaining	______	______
Asking for information	*1*	______
Giving information	______	______
Correcting information	______	______
Giving advice	______	______

1 I would also be grateful if you could inform me of the prices and dates of your two-week and one-month intensive courses.

2 You really shouldn't buy anything in the markets there – it's all poor quality stuff and far too expensive.

3 I am writing to draw your attention to several inaccuracies contained in your article on secondary schools in Greece.

4 And I do think you could have phoned me to tell me you weren't coming – I wasted the whole morning waiting for you!

5 With regard to the number of children in our group, we estimate that there will be approximately 12 boys and 12 girls, all aged 15 and under.

6 I thought your article was great, but I noticed a few things which were wrong, so I thought I'd better write and tell you about them before you send it off.

7 Moreover, when the food eventually arrived, the fish was undercooked and we had to ask one of your waiters to take it back to the kitchen.

8 Owing to the high frequency of thefts in the area, we would strongly advise you not to carry large amounts of cash with you.

9 I reckon it'll take us about two hours to get to your place, so we should see you at about 3 o'clock.

10 Can you let me know what time you think you'll be arriving?

2 Some of the words and expressions have been underlined in the sentences above. Match each formal word or expression with its informal equivalent and write them both in the table below. There is an example at the beginning.

Formal	Informal
1 inform me	*10 let me know*
______	______
______	______
______	______
______	______

FCE Part 2

Informal letters

Informal letters: pages 10 and 11 of the Coursebook

1 Read the following Writing Part 1 instructions.

You have just received a letter from your British penfriend, accepting your invitation to come and stay with you just after Christmas. Read the extract from the letter below, and then write a reply to your friend, answering his questions and telling him what plans you have for when he comes to visit.

Thanks very much for the invitation to stay with your family for a few days after Christmas - of course I'd love to come!

I've already found out about flights, and I could arrive at 12.30 midday on the 27th December. As you know, I've never been abroad during the Christmas holidays so I have no idea what to expect. What kinds of things do you normally do then? And what's the weather like there at that time of year? Let me know if there are any special clothes I should bring with me.

2 Note that for this task you have to tell your penfriend about:

a the kinds of things you normally do at that time
b any special clothes he needs to bring
c the plans you have for when he comes to stay.

Read the model below and decide in which paragraph each of these three points is mentioned. Write each letter **a**, **b** and **c** next to the corresponding paragraph, **1**, **2** or **3**.

Dear Roger

Beginning
Thanks a lot for your letter - it was great to hear from you again and we're delighted you can come and stay with us.

Paragraph 1
As you can imagine, everything's very quiet here then. We normally spend the time just relaxing at home, getting over all the celebrations and finishing off the Christmas food! We either read or play games, and occasionally we go out for a walk in the snow.

Paragraph 2
When you're here, though, we'd like to take you to the mountains for a few days - they're really beautiful at this time of the year. We can go cross-country skiing during the day and then in the evenings we can try out the different restaurants. The area is famous for its good food.

Paragraph 3
The temperatures drop to minus 10° in December, so make sure you bring some warm clothes. A pair of walking boots would be ideal, as well as some waterproof trousers if you have them - just in case you fall over in the snow!

Ending
That's all for now, then. We'll see you at the airport on the 27th.
Best wishes
Katrin

3 Write your own letter to a British penfriend who is coming to stay with you for the first time for **a week in August**. Include the same points, **a**, **b** and **c**, as in the letter above and follow the same paragraph plan. Write your letter in **120–180** words.

Don't forget!

Plan your letter before you write it. Use some of the informal language and linkers from page 10 of the Coursebook.

2 High energy

Reading

FCE Part 1

Multiple matching

1 You are going to read an interview with Linford Christie, who used to be a professional athlete. The eight questions which the interviewer asked have been removed from the article. Choose from the questions **A–I** the one which fits each space **(1–7)**. There is one extra question which you do not need to use. There is an example at the beginning **(0)**.

A Has the Internet changed the nature of sport?
B What makes a winner?
C What do you do now that you're retired?
D What's your most useful piece of equipment?
E Has technology made sport too serious?
F How do nerves affect you?
G Do you run faster if you're angry?
H How do you prepare for an important race?
I Did you always want to be a professional athlete?

Linford Christie

0 I

I didn't know I was going to be one until quite late on. I only became a professional when I was 25, which is quite unusual. If I'd known before, I'd have started training earlier. My dad wanted me to be an electrician, but like everyone else I wanted to be a footballer.

1 ____

You certainly have to be in good physical condition. If you train hard, you can be a world-class distance runner, but you have to be born a champion sprinter. I run 105 metres. Most people run 95 and then slow down, but that is how you lose a race. My coach always taught me to keep on running through the finishing line.

2 ____

They're something a good sprinter has to learn to live with. Sometimes they start a week before a race: you think about it and your heart goes faster. After a while, you learn to control them and just get a little **edgy** a couple of hours before the race.

3 ____

Sprinting is an aggressive sport, but the aggression has to be controlled. Too much anger and you become tense, and that's the worst thing for a runner. Everyone has their own way of preparing themselves mentally for a race, but you can't afford **to get too worked up** or you'll lose.

4 ____

I'm not into it myself because you can become too addicted. But it does make it easier to get information.You can consult different web pages to find out about legal herbs and vitamins which will help you run better, or which competitions your colleagues are taking part in and what times they do. But I don't use it as much as some people.

5 ____

Yes, to a certain extent it has, and I think that sometimes we rely on it too much. I was disqualified for three false starts in the Atlanta Olympics, thanks to a machine which said I'd left the starting blocks too early. Machines have dehumanised sport and taken some of the fun out of it, but having said that, I do think they are very useful.

6 ____

Without a doubt it's my start machine, a kind of electronic stopwatch, which I got in 1990 for £1,500. **It was pricey** even then but it was vital for my running career. In the first twelve months I had it, I improved my time over 60m from 6.8 seconds to 6.6. It may not sound very much, but in athletics it can make the difference between a winner and a runner-up.

7 ____

I still train and run a little, but I've been doing other things as well: presenting TV sports programmes, advertising, modelling, as well as running my company Nuff Respect, which helps to market and manage sports people. I always think like a competitor, because it's the only way I can succeed. I have **to be on the go** all the time; I can't just sit doing nothing.

2 The informal words and expressions in **1–5** below appear in **bold** in the text. Use the context to help you decide on the most appropriate meaning, **A**, **B**, **C** or **D**, for each one as it appears in the text. The paragraph numbers are given in brackets.

1 edgy (2)
A faster
B tired
C nervous
D worried

2 to get too worked up (3)
A to work too hard
B to do too many things at the same time
C to get too angry
D to earn too much money

3 I'm not into it myself (4)
A I haven't got it.
B I'm not interested in it.
C I never use it.
D I don't worry about it.

4 It was pricey (6)
A I won it in a competition.
B It was very useful.
C I bought it second-hand.
D It cost a lot of money.

5 to be on the go (7)
A to be busy
B to compete in races
C to leave
D to be successful

Vocabulary

Wordlist on page 202 of the Coursebook

A Music

Can you identify each of the following musical instruments?

1
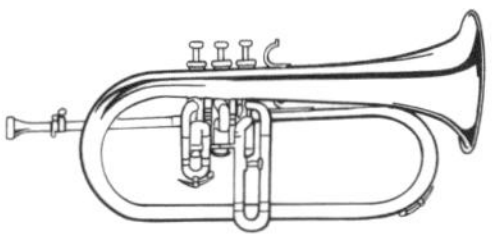
____

2
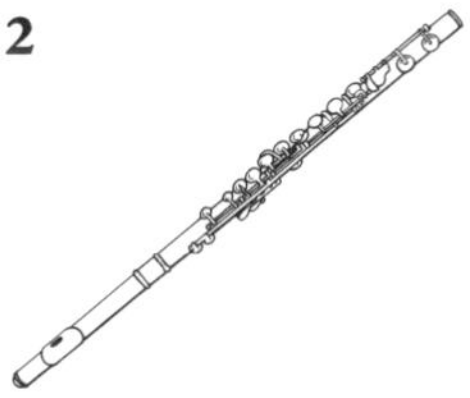
____

3

____

4
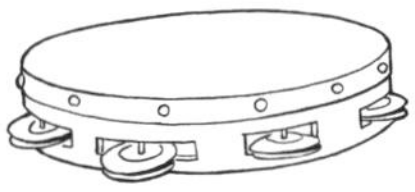
____

5
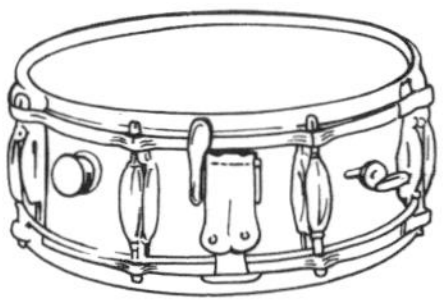
____

6

____

7
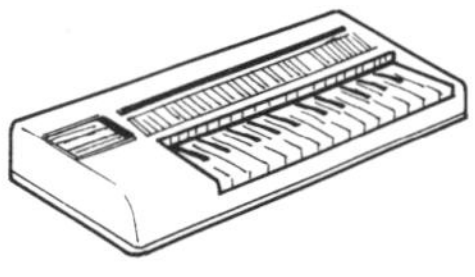
____

8

____

B Sport

1 Write the words for the people who do each of the following sports.

Example:
surfing *surfer*

a athletics ________
b basketball ________
c cycling ________
d golf ________
e gymnastics ________
f skiing ________
g snowboarding ________
h tennis ________

2 Match the sports in column **A** with the places in column **B**.

A		B
1 motor-racing	*circuit*	rink
2 football	________	court
3 athletics	________	slope
4 ski	________	pool
5 swimming	________	track
6 golf	________	pitch
7 tennis	________	circuit
8 ice-skating	________	course

3 In questions **1–8** choose the best answer **A**, **B**, **C** or **D** to complete these sentences.

1 He was given a full set of golf ________ as a retirement present.
A bats **B** clubs **C** sticks **D** posts

2 Only five seconds separated the winner from the ________ in this year's London marathon.
A opponent **B** failure **C** loser **D** runner-up

3 Olympiakos ________ 0–0 with Real Madrid in the first leg of the semi-final in Athens.
A drew **B** equalled **C** equalized **D** shared

4 Second Division football ________ get paid very little in my country.
A judges **B** arbitrators **C** referees **D** umpires

5 We are expecting over 300 surfers to take ________ in this year's national surfing championship.
A place **B** up **C** part **D** competition

6 I've never really enjoyed ________ sport.
A going in **B** taking up **C** practising **D** doing

7 The home side ________ 76–75 in a thrilling game of basketball.
A won **B** beat **C** scored **D** marked

8 The players were cheered by their ________ as they came off the pitch.
A audience **B** supporters **C** viewers **D** public

Language focus

Grammar reference on page 206 of the Coursebook

A Indirect questions

Complete these sentences by putting the words in the right order.

1 doing/have/me/been/you/telling/what/recently
Would you mind ______________________________?

2 something/can/cold/drink/where/I/to/get
Does anybody know ______________________________?

3 party/time/week/the/are/what/you/coming/to/next
Could you tell me ______________________________?

4 homework/did/the/not/me/you/to/do/why
Could you explain ______________________________?

5 interested/Friday/playing/if/in/on/are/tennis/you
We'd like to know ______________________________.

6 he/living/does/a/for/what
I wonder ______________________________.

B Gerunds and infinitives

Complete each of the following spaces with either the gerund or the infinitive of the word in brackets.

1 I don't mind ___________ (look) after the neighbour's cat for a week, but I refuse ___________ (have) it here in the house.

2 At first I was really keen on the idea of ___________ (learn) ___________ (speak) Swahili, but now I'm beginning ___________ (think) it's a bit of a waste of time.

3 There appeared ___________ (be) no one in the house. Pickering considered ___________ (climb) through one of the open windows but if he did this, he risked ___________ (attract) the attention of the neighbours. He decided ___________ (wait) until it was dark.

4 Please stop ___________ (make) so much noise. I'm trying ___________ (concentrate).

5 I really don't feel like ___________ (go) out tonight. I'd prefer ___________ (stay) in and watch a video.

6 ___________ (give) up chocolate is a good idea, but if you intend ___________ (lose) ten kilos in three months you'll have to do a lot more than that!

7 I'm delighted ___________ (hear) you're coming to the wedding. Rachel and I are certainly both looking forward to ___________ (see) you again.

8 I've been meaning ___________ (paint) the front door for ages, but I keep ___________ (forget) ___________ (buy) the paint.

9 We'd really like ___________ (live) in the city centre but it's virtually impossible ___________ (find) a three-bedroomed flat at a price we can afford ___________ (pay).

10 I left school when I was 16 ___________ (work) in my father's firm, but now I regret not ___________ (go) to university.

Use of English

FCE Part 2

Open cloze: Prepositions

Complete each of the following spaces with a suitable preposition. The first one has been done for you **(0)**.

Heavy musicians

I've never been particularly fond **(0)** _of_ heavy metal music, but my dad's a real fan. He used to go and see groups play **(1)** ______ concert all the time when he was a teenager, and when he found out that one of his favourite live bands, 'Black Purple', was going **(2)** ______ tour again, he just had to get tickets. He told me the lead vocalist was famous **(3)** ______ being a bit crazy and that he used to jump off the stage **(4)** ______ the audience. I knew they'd had a few records **(5)** ______ the charts **(6)** ______ the seventies, and the two or three tracks I'd heard **(7)** ______ the radio didn't sound too bad, so when my dad asked me to go with him I agreed.
When they came **(8)** ______ stage I began to realize I'd made a big mistake. All the members of the band were **(9)** ______ least 60 years old, they all looked really **(10)** ______ of condition and they produced some of the worst sounds I've ever heard. The guitarists were either extremely untalented or their instruments just weren't **(11)** ______ tune. The drummer looked completely uninterested **(12)** ______ everything and seemed to be playing the same beat over and over again. And as for the lead vocalist, he was quite good **(13)** ______ jumping up and down, but he certainly couldn't sing. I got fed up **(14)** ______ it all after about three songs and wanted to go home, but my dad made me stay **(15)** ______ the end.

FCE Part 3

Transformations

Complete the second sentence so that it has a similar meaning to the first sentence, using the word given. **Do not change the word given.** You must use between two and five words, including the word given. There is an example at the beginning **(0)**.

0 Rita, could I borrow your dictionary?
mind
Rita, *would you mind lending* ______ me your dictionary?

1 It's impossible for me not to laugh when he starts singing.
help
I can't ______ when he starts singing.

2 I'm going to start playing golf this year.
take
I'm going ______ this year.

3 I don't like playing football very much.
keen
I ______ playing football.

4 I hate it when I'm ill.
stand
I ______ ill.

5 Andrea doesn't usually arrive late.
unusual
It ______ arrive late.

6 Do you know where they're going to hold the Olympic Games in 2008?
place
Do you know where the Olympic Games are going
______ in 2008?

7 I can't play tennis very well.
good
I ______ playing tennis.

FCE Part 5

Word formation

Use the word given in capitals at the end of each line to form a word that fits the space. The word you need may be an adjective, an adverb, a noun or the past tense of a verb. All of the words require a prefix.

1 Most of what you've written in your composition has nothing to do with the question and is therefore ______ . **RELEVANT**

2 There was some ______ about who should be team captain. **AGREE**

3 You obviously ______ when I set the homework. You've done the wrong exercise. **UNDERSTAND**

4 He claimed he had won the lottery, though most people who knew him suspected he had obtained the money ______ . **HONEST**

5 Derek is so ______ . You can never trust him to arrive on time for anything. **RELY**

6 His childish and ______ behaviour often gets him into trouble at school. **MATURE**

7 I keep telling you you're ______ ; those trousers are far too tight for you now! **WEIGH**

8 The potatoes are ______ ; you should have boiled them for a bit longer. **COOK**

9 The parents, who had left the two young children alone in the house, were accused of behaving ______ . **RESPONSIBLE**

10 He always asks me what I think he should do. He seems ______ of making his own decisions. **CAPABLE**

Writing

FCE Part 1

Transactional letters

Read the following Writing Part 1 question and do the related tasks in **A–D** below.

You would like to go on a short skiing holiday in winter. Your friend Nick, who went skiing in Scotland last year, has sent you the following advertisement for the resort he stayed at. Read the advertisement and the notes you have made, then write a letter to Nick asking for more information.

Write a **letter** of between **120–180** words in an appropriate style. Do not write any addresses.

SKIING IN SCOTLAND

at the Nevis Range ski resort
close to Ben Nevis, Britain's highest mountain.
Only a train journey away! — *cheaper by bus?*

Nevis Range offers the best skiing in Scotland with 12 lifts and 40 downhill runs up to two km long. Runs are wide and varied with easy 'green' runs through to very difficult 'black' ones. — *How many?*

Our three or five day package includes:

- accommodation in centrally heated cabins
- full board
- lift pass

daily classes also available — *useful?* *good instructors?*

Price: £150 three days
£195 five days

Caledonian Spirit Ltd
Fort William, Scotland
Tel: 01397 27716

ask about cost of ski hire

A Formal and informal style

In **1–10** below, decide which of the two sentences, **a** or **b**, is written in a more informal style and put a tick (✓) next to it.

1 a Firstly, as I'm not an experienced skier, I'd really like to know how many green runs there are.

b Firstly, owing to the fact that I am not an experienced skier, I am particularly interested to know how many green runs there are.

2 a And can you remember if the skis cost a lot to hire?

b In addition to this, could you give me some information on the cost of equipment hire?

3 a I am writing in response to the advertisement you sent me about skiing in Nevis Range.

b Thanks for sending me the advert about skiing in Nevis Range.

4 a Finally, I only intend to spend three days skiing. I would therefore like to know whether I would benefit from having classes.
b Finally, I'm only planning to go skiing for three days, so I'd like to know if you think it's worth having classes.

5 a Thank you in anticipation for your help. I look forward to hearing from you soon.
b Thanks for all your help. Write back soon.

6 a I wanted to ask you some questions about costs, as well.
b In addition, I would like to have further details about costs.

7 a However, before I book, I would be grateful if you could answer some queries which I have.
b But before I book, there are a few things I'd like to ask you.

8 a Does the resort employ fully qualified instructors?
b I suppose it depends on the instructors – were they good?

9 a It sounds just the sort of place I'm looking for.
b I feel it would be particularly suited to my needs.

10 a Do you think I'd save much by getting the bus from London instead of the train?
b In your opinion, would the cost of bus travel from London be a great deal cheaper than a train journey?

B An informal letter

Now reconstruct the informal letter by putting the sentences you have ticked in a logical order. Write out the letter in the space provided. Organize the letter into logical paragraphs. The first sentence **(3b)** has been written for you.

Dear Nick

Thanks for sending me the advert about skiing in NevisRange.

All the best

Caroline

C Building on the information given

Candidates who write good answers to Part 1 questions attempt to build on the information given by adding relevant points of their own.

Read the following three sentences and decide at which point in the letter in B above they could each go.

1 I expect you went on all the black runs, but they'd be much too difficult for me.
2 As you know, I haven't got much money at the moment, so the holiday needs to be as cheap as possible.
3 If they're too expensive, I'll ask a friend to lend me hers.

D Linking words and expressions

Look back at the sentences in A on pages 15 and 16 and find the formal equivalents for the following informal linking words and expressions.

Informal	Formal
as well	*in addition*
and	________
as	________
so	________
but	________

E Writing task

Answer the following Part 1 question.

You are studying English in London and you have just received a letter from your friend, Ken, who is a sailing instructor on the south coast. Read the following extract from the letter together with the notes you have made. Then write to your friend asking for more information.

and I'm really enjoying the job.

By the way, we're going to run weekend sailing courses for complete beginners. Why don't you come down to Hamble and do one? You've always said you wanted to learn to sail, so this would be an ideal opportunity. And after only a few weekends you could get your RYA 2 certificate.

how many?

more details, please

We start the first one next month - let me know if you're interested.

Best wishes

Ken

Don't forget to ask:
- *need to be a good swimmer?*
- *possible to stay at your house?*
- *number of hours each day?*

Write a **letter** of between **120–180** words in an appropriate style. Do not write any addresses.

Don't forget!

You're writing to a friend, so use informal language. Look again at pages 10 and 11 of the Coursebook for information about writing informal letters.

3 A change for the better?

Reading

FCE Part 4

Multiple matching

1 You are going to read a magazine article in which people are interviewed about technology. Read through the six texts quite quickly and decide:

a which of the people speak positively about technology. ____________

b which of them have a more negative opinion. ____________

Technology and you

Like it or not, technology is a fact of life. But what do you think of it all? June Avery asked some of our readers.

A Angela

My mother bought me a microwave oven recently. I couldn't believe it – like me, she was never very keen on modern technology and there she was, buying me a microwave. I live on my own in a one-bedroomed flat and it just about fits into the corner of my tiny kitchen. I have to admit, it's extremely handy, particularly as I don't have a great deal of time to cook when I get home from work. I virtually depend on it now.

B Barbara

First of all, of course, we got a PC, partly because it's so useful for work, but also, I suppose, because everyone else seemed to have one. That was fine for a couple of years, but then the kids took it over with their computer games, so we got ourselves a laptop for our own exclusive use. It doesn't take up much room, and being portable we can use it in any part of the house. After that, we just couldn't help ourselves every time a new piece of technology came out; a palm top or personal organizer, a digital video camera, a video mobile phone – we just had to have it. And the more things we buy, of course, the more we want.

C Carol

Our house is full of all the latest gadgets. In the kitchen alone we've got an electric carving knife, a yoghurt maker, an automatic potato peeler, a bread making machine and a device for taking the stones out of peaches without cutting them open. As far as I'm concerned, though, they're a waste of time. They're always going wrong and my husband keeps having to mend them. I think they're more trouble than they're worth but he seems to think we couldn't get by without them.

D Dorothy

Like most people we have our fair share of appliances. I couldn't imagine living without a freezer or a washing machine; and who hasn't got a cooker or a fridge nowadays? I know people had to cope without these things 40 or 50 years ago, but the world was a different place then, wasn't it? Everything's so much faster now, and in some families men and women work just as many hours as each other away from home. We couldn't do that *and* bring up children without the support of all these labour-saving devices.

E Elsie

We're a bit too old for all this technology. A friend of ours says we should be on the Internet but I can't see why, and to be honest I'd be too scared to use it. It's all too fast for me. In the old days everything used to be so much more simple and people seemed to spend a lot more time chatting to each other.

F Florence

The Internet has revolutionised people's lives, and we're no exception. We use it for everything, especially shopping. It's so much more convenient than actually going to the shops. Of course, you don't get the same personal treatment, but now that most people go to supermarkets and these large shopping centres, I really don't think you get much of that anyway nowadays. Of course, there are some things we pop out to buy such as bread or milk, but generally, once a month we make an order from the nearest hypermarket via the Internet and no more than a couple of hours later it's all packed away in the fridge or the freezer.

2 For questions **1–15**, choose from the people **(A–F)**. The people may be chosen more than once. When more than one answer is required, these may be given in any order. There is an example at the beginning **(0)**.

Which of the people A–F

was surprised by another person's actions?	**0** *A*
often has problems with machines?	**1**
finds it impossible to resist buying the latest technology?	**2**
is frightened of some of the new technology?	**3**
doesn't feel she is any different from other people?	**4**
likes the speed with which things can be done?	**5** **6**
feels that technology is important in the modern-day family?	**7**
doesn't agree with someone else in the family?	**8**
has changed her way of thinking?	**9**
doesn't like the fact that people talk to each other less now?	**10**
wanted to be the same as other people?	**11**
doesn't have much room for domestic appliances?	**12**
says that the way we live has changed?	**13** **14** **15**

3 Each of the following extracts from the reading texts contains a phrasal verb. Match each verb to an equivalent word or explanation.

Barbara

1 then the kids **took** it **over** with their computer games ...
2 It doesn't **take up** much room ...
3 every time a new piece of technology **came out** ...

Carol

4 he seems to think we couldn't **get by** without them.

Dorothy

5 We couldn't do that *and* **bring up** children ...

a occupy
b raise; care for a child until it is an adult
c be sold to the public for the first time
d manage to survive or live
e get control of (from somebody else)

4 Complete each of the following spaces with the correct form of one of the phrasal verbs from exercise 3.

1 We had to sell the car last year and we're finding it difficult to ____________ without it.

2 A new computer magazine called *Log On* ____________ last month; they gave away a free computer game with the first copy.

3 We're going to get some new speakers for this music centre; these ones ____________ too much space.

4 My parents ____________ me ____________ to tell the truth and I'm grateful that they did.

5 When our daughter left home, my husband ____________ her bedroom and converted it into an office.

Vocabulary

Wordlist on page 203 of Coursebook

Technology

Across

1 adjective meaning 'useful'; a _____ device
3 abbreviation: digital technology which is replacing video
7 a computer which is 8 down
9 having typed your document on a computer, you can save it and/or print it _____ .
10 you can do this in the sea and on the World Wide Web
11 preposition: _____ TV, _____ the radio, _____ the phone, _____ the Net
12 'to _____ on' to the Net means 'to gain access' to it
13 with cable and _____ TV, many more channels and programmes are available

Down

1 you need these to listen to your Discman or Walkman
2 if you need the emergency services in Britain, the number to _____ is 999
4 an adjective to describe things such as contact lenses, cutlery and cups that you throw away after use
5 in order to change TV channels from the comfort of your sofa, you use a _____ control
6 abbreviation for 'information technology'
8 adjective to describe a device, machine etc which you can carry
10 a music _____ consists of a CD player, tape recorder, radio and sometimes a turntable

Language focus

Grammar reference on pages 207 and 208 of the Coursebook

A Articles

In the following sentences decide which spaces require an article. Write *a, an,* or *the* or leave the space blank.

1 ______ electric toaster was invented over ______ hundred years ago, although ______ consumers only began to show interest in it in ______ nineteen thirties.

2 You can take ______ dogs and ______ other pets into ______ Britain but they have to have ______ passport and wear ______ microchip under their skin. ______ 'passport' is in fact ______ health certificate and ______ microchip contains ______ information such as ______ address of the pet and its telephone number.

3 When we were on ______ holiday in ______ mountains last week we saw ______ bear.

4 She works as ______ teacher in ______ school for ______ blind in Ireland. ______ school has over ______ thousand pupils.

5 Leslie: 'I'm looking forward to this concert. Have you got ______ tickets?
Linda: 'Oh no! I've left them at ______ home. Don't worry, though. I'll get ______ taxi – I can be there and back in half ______ hour.'

B Comparisons

Complete each of the spaces in **1–10** with the correct form of one of the adjectives from the box. You may have to use the comparative or superlative form or you may not need to make any change at all.

soon	early	boring	good	careful	tired	fast	hard	quiet	hot

1 I knew the exam would be difficult, but I didn't expect it to be as ____________ as that.

2 Last summer was the ____________ since records began, with temperatures reaching 40° in some parts of Britain.

3 There are too many mistakes in this composition. You need to be a lot ____________ .

4 He was very ill last week, but I'm pleased to say he seems to be getting ____________ now.

5 I look forward to hearing from you as ____________ as possible.

6 That was the ____________ film I've ever seen. I nearly fell asleep near the end.

7 The later you go to bed, the ____________ you'll feel tomorrow.

8 We were the first guests to arrive at the party. We got there half an hour ____________ than anybody else.

9 The cheetah, which can run at a speed of 110 kilometres an hour, is the ____________ animal in the world.

10 Life in the countryside is so much ____________ than in the city; no traffic, no crowds and no neighbours!

C Comparative expressions

Match a line of dialogue on the left with an appropriate response on the right.

1 Don't get upset. You shouldn't lose your temper with him.
2 I was in a hurry to leave and I fell over on the stairs.
3 Amazing, Andy! How did you do that?
4 Do you understand what you have to do?
5 He said he'd phone me, but he hasn't.

a More or less.
b That's easier said than done.
c He will, sooner or later.
d More haste less speed.
e More by luck than judgement.

D Error correction

1 Read **1–5** below and match each paragraph to one of the following inventions.

video	compass	radar	Walkman	space blanket

1 This invention <u>which</u> completely changed the lives of music-lovers around the world. At first Sony executives thought the idea of people walking round with headphones on their heads would not be a success. But however its creator, Akio Morita, always knew that the portable device, more smaller than a paperback book, would be popular.

2 This device was the most of important navigation instrument to be invented in the last millennium. Originally, sailors used the position of the Sun and the North Star to can know which way they were going, but clouds often caused them to lose their way. This invention made possible the exploration of distant lands, including America, probably the most significant of event of civilisation of the past one thousand years.

3 The first machines were built in the 1950s but for many years its cost limited its use to the television and film industry. By the early 1980s significantly very cheaper versions were introduced and have since become nearly as most common as television sets. Now viewers can watch their favourite programmes whenever they choose and as more often as they like.

4 This is made from a material called Mylar, a type of the plastic, covered with a microscopically thin film of metal. It is used to, for example, for exhausted marathon runners or for keeping mountaineers warm. The material existed in the 1950s but its production became much more sophisticated as a result of the man's efforts to land on the Moon in the following decade.

5 The name of this invention comes from the phrase, 'radio detection and ranging' and is used for to detect the presence of objects and calculate their distance, as well as their size, shape and speed. Although originally developed as an instrument as of war, it is now used for controlling air traffic and predicting the weather. In addition to, it has important applications in astronomical research.

2 Each of the descriptions has **three words** which should not be there. Find the words and underline them. The first one has been done for you.

Use of English

FCE Part 3

Transformations

Complete the second sentence so that it has a similar meaning to the first sentence, using the word given. **Do not change the word given.** You must use between two and five words. There is an example at the beginning **(0)**.

0 My brother isn't quite as tall as me.
slightly
My brother is *slightly shorter than* ______ me.

1 This exercise is much easier than the last one.
nearly
This exercise is ______ as the last one.

2 There are more boys than girls in our class.
as
There are ______ as boys in our class.

3 All the other chairs in the room are more comfortable than this one.
comfortable
This is the ______ the room.

4 I eat more if I smoke less.
the
The less ______ I eat.

5 I live nearer to the school than Costas.
from
Costas ______ the school than I do.

6 I did far better than Chris in the exam.
much
Chris ______ me in the exam.

7 James earns more than me.
as
I do ______ James does.

8 I've never known anyone as clever as Hilary.
person
Hilary is ______ ever known.

FCE Part 2

Open cloze

1 Read the text through quickly, ignoring the spaces, and decide which sentence best summarizes the paragraph.

a Printing on paper will soon be a thing of the past.
b Printers of the future will use a variety of materials.
c New printing techniques will revolutionise the car industry.

2 Now read the text again and complete each space with one word.

Those of us who have **(0)** *a* computer with access to the Net are all **(1)** __________ to printing out information we have found **(2)** __________ . With a single click, we can send **(3)** __________ to the printer on our desktop and obtain a perfect reproduction. **(4)** __________ next generation of home printers, however, will be printing out not just words and pictures, but 3-D objects as **(5)** __________ . If you are surfing the Net and you see a picture of a doll that would **(6)** __________ perfect for a child's birthday present, click **(7)** __________ it and an exact reproduction will emerge from your domestic fabricator in a matter of minutes. Experts believe this will happen sooner rather than **(8)** __________ . They say that in just a few years from now, we will be producing 3-D fax machines for **(9)** __________ than £1,000 – perhaps even no more than £750 – and they will be available in your local high-street store. **(10)** __________ machines will at first be limited to producing plastic objects, such as **(11)** __________ individualised mobile phone case. However, **(12)** __________ ultimate goal is a 3-D fax machine **(13)** __________ can 'print' using materials such as metals or ceramics. If the technology can be made cheap, you could see a replacement part for your car emerge from the equivalent of a printer **(14)** __________ smoothly as a picture **(15)** __________ today.

FCE Part 5

Word formation

Use the word given in capitals at the end of each line to form a word that fits in the space in the same line. There is an example at the beginning **(0)**.

The microwave oven

Perhaps the most **(0)** *useful* and convenient of all domestic appliances **USE**
is the microwave oven. You do not need to be a **(1)** __________ **SKILL**
cook or a **(2)** __________ genius to operate one, and you can produce **TECHNOLOGY**
extremely **(3)** __________ meals at the touch of a button. Many of **TASTE**
us would now feel rather **(4)** __________ and unable to cope **HELP**
without one. The man we have to thank for this modern cooking
miracle is **(5)** __________ , Percy LeBaron Spencer, who **INVENT**
manufactured the Radar Range oven for industrial use in 1945.
Ten years **(6)** __________ the first domestic microwave made its **LATE**
(7) __________ . This rather bulky contraption needed an **APPEAR**
(8) __________ and a plumber to install it and was the same size **ELECTRIC**
as a fridge. At over $1,000 in 1955, it was not immediately
(9) __________ . Not until 1967, when the countertop model became **SUCCEED**
(10) __________ available, did sales start to improve. **WIDE**

Writing

FCE Part 2

Articles and compositions

1 Read the following two Writing Part 2 questions.

1 You have been doing a class project on technology in the home. Your teacher has asked you to write a composition giving your opinions on the following statement:
Modern domestic appliances and devices do not make us happier.
Write your **composition**.

2 You see this notice in an international magazine.

> **Technology in the Home**
>
> Technology is everywhere today, and especially in the home. We d like you, the readers, to write a short article telling us which **two** modern domestic appliances or devices you would find it most difficult to live without — not forgetting, of course, to say why.
>
> The three best articles will be published in our magazine.

Write your **article**.

2 Decide which of the paragraphs below were written in answer to the article, and which form part of the composition. Rearrange each answer in the correct order and put the corresponding letters in the table. Pay close attention to the style of the language used and the linking words.

	Composition	Article
Paragraph 1	*e*	______
Paragraph 2	______	______
Paragraph 3	______	______
Paragraph 4	______	______

a Firstly, there's the cooker, which keeps me in the kitchen for far too long. If I didn't have to cook, I could do a million and one more interesting things. But we all have to eat, and we couldn't get by on just salads and cold meat. Of course, we have a microwave, but the meals it produces just aren't as tasty as those from a conventional oven.

b On the other hand, some modern technology has made our lives less interesting than before. Food which has been taken from the freezer and heated in a microwave is not as tasty as fresh food cooked in a conventional oven. Moreover, the reason many people buy these labour-saving devices is to enable them to spend more time working, which does not necessarily make them happier.

c So it seems the things we most need are not always the things we most love.

d In conclusion, although technology has made life easier in the home, it is not necessarily the key to happiness.

e Nowadays, many people have a wide range of appliances and devices in their home, all of which are designed to make life easier. However, they also have some disadvantages.

f <u>A love-hate relationship</u>
Can you imagine an object in your house which you dislike having to use but which you know you couldn't do without? I can think of two, and just hearing their names mentioned makes me feel depressed.

g On the one hand, they have reduced the amount of time required to complete domestic chores. Cleaning and ironing, for example, can be done far more quickly and efficiently than fifty years ago. In addition, some inventions have meant that certain tasks no longer have to be performed. Washing up is almost extinct in households with a dishwasher, and thanks to the microwave, cooking is no more than pushing a button.

h And perhaps worse than the cooker is the iron. The same monotonous action, forwards and backwards, hour after hour, whether it's a shirt or a skirt, shorts or trousers. No one in my family likes ironing, but no one would consider wearing clothes or sleeping between sheets which have not first been ironed.

3 Look back at the two answers in 2 and decide which of the features below occur in the article and which are used in the composition. Put a tick (✓) or a cross (✗) in the relevant column and give examples, if appropriate. The first one has been done for you.

	Composition	Article
Contractions	✗	✓ *couldn't, there's, didn't*
Phrasal verbs		
Formal linkers		
Informal linkers		
Direct questions		

4 You are going to write your own article in answer to question **2**. Decide which two items you want to write about and plan your article using the following advice.

Title	Think of a title which will attract the reader's attention. You might like to do this when you have finished writing your article. Try to make it relevant to the whole article.
Paragraph 1	Introduction. Interest and involve your reader from the start. You could ask a direct question or make a surprising statement. You could draw attention to the similarities or differences between your two items, and/or make a general statement about how important they are to you.
Paragraph 2	Talk about your first item and why you could not live without it.
Paragraph 3	Now do the same for the second item.
Paragraph 4	Conclusion. End with a short statement or a question which summarizes your feelings and/or leaves the reader something to think about.

5 Write your **article** in **120–180** words. Make sure you write in an appropriate style, using those features which you ticked for articles in exercise 3 above.

For more help with writing articles see page 200 of the Coursebook.

4 A good story

Reading

FCE Part 2

Multiple choice

1 You are going to read a magazine article about the effects of fame. For questions **1–7**, choose the answer (**A**, **B**, **C** or **D**) which you think best fits according to the text.

What Price Fame?

How do film stars cope with being famous? Does fame bring happiness? Rory Taylor takes a closer look at stardom and its effects on those lucky enough to have it.

After more than 20 years in the film industry Mel Gibson says that the biggest lesson he's learned as an actor has been how important it is to have a loving family at his side. 'When I started out in my career I was often referred to as "the sexiest man in the world" or some such nonsense. At the time, though, it went to my head and I really took to being a celebrity. However, after the initial euphoria I found that not only was I spending long periods away from home but I never had any time to myself, none of which made me particularly happy.' His wife Robyn saw what was happening and came to the rescue; she simply told him to 'stop, come home and take some time off.'

But Mel Gibson thinks it's ten times worse for today's young stars. He believes that the new breed of heart-throbs such as Brad Pitt and Leonardo DiCaprio have it much harder than he ever did. 'The youngsters today receive constant attention from the media, which means they can't do anything without seeing their picture all over the front page the next day.'

The experience of Cameron Diaz bears witness to that. All the time she was dating Matt Dillon she never felt her personal life was her own. 'After a while we both got used to being chased by photographers, and having every aspect of our relationship analysed by the media. But it meant we could never really lead a normal life together.' The pressures of working together with Dillon on *There's Something About Mary* were probably as much to blame for their painful and much publicised break-up as the sensation-seeking journalists, but all the same, Cameron has resolved to be more guarded about her private life and she now gives as little away as possible about her relationships.

Wild man of comedy, Jim Carrey, also complains about the lack of privacy. He remembers with anger the time he took some family photographs to be developed in a shop close to his $4 million Los Angeles home. 'Two weeks later they were in the local newspaper. Someone in the shop obviously made a lot of money out of them.' For Carrey, being a famous actor also means being a diplomat. 'People may come up to you in the street when you're in a really bad mood, and you have to talk to them as if you were delighted to see them. If not, word gets round that you're a miserable human being and that's how you're remembered.'

Bruce Willis feels that too much importance is attached to what's written in magazine articles, since most of it's untrue anyway. He firmly believes he has a right to protect himself and his family from over-inquisitive reporters. 'If the paparazzi start taking photos of my children and asking them questions, I just get in the way and teach them a few manners. Of course, they don't take too kindly to this, and the public is given the impression from what they read that I'm arrogant and rude. It's all very frustrating.'

Frustrating it may be, but how sorry should we feel for people like Willis? Michael Douglas and Catherine Zeta-Jones certainly can't complain about journalists: it is said they were paid £1 million by *OK!* magazine for allowing its photographers to take exclusive pictures of their wedding. Of course, being in the public eye does have its drawbacks, but these are nothing compared with the positive aspects of fame. After all, if the publicity and pressure of fame get too much for the Douglas family, they can always escape to Michael's large house on the beautiful Mediterranean island of Mallorca. Fame is a wonderful thing – as long as you can afford to get away from it!

1 What are we told about Mel Gibson's attitude to fame?
A It has taught him a lot about life.
B He enjoyed it at first.
C It has helped to make him happy.
D Fame is not important to him.

2 What does the author mean when he says that the experience of Cameron Diaz 'bears witness to that' in line 21?
A She was with Brad Pitt and Leonardo DiCaprio when they were photographed.
B She understands what it's like to be a photographer.
C What happened to her proves that young film stars have no privacy.
D Her experience was worse than that of Brad Pitt and Leonardo DiCaprio.

3 What, according to the writer, caused Cameron Diaz and Matt Dillon to end their relationship?
A Their appearance together in a film.
B Cameron Diaz had a relationship with someone else.
C A combination of reasons.
D The attentions of the media.

4 Jim Carrey was angry about the photographs because
A they took a long time to develop.
B they were very expensive to develop.
C the shop was closed for a long time.
D his privacy was not respected.

5 What does Jim Carrey say about being recognized in the street?
A He sometimes has to hide his true feelings.
B He finds it very irritating.
C He is always pleased to meet people.
D It is a sign that people have not forgotten him.

6 What does 'they' in line 52 refer to?
A his children
B the paparazzi
C photos
D the public

7 What is the author's opinion of the rich and famous?
A He thinks they are paid too much.
B He thinks we should feel sorry for them.
C He thinks their lifestyle has more advantages than disadvantages.
D He thinks they complain too much.

2 Write a corresponding noun form for the following adjectives. All the nouns appear in the reading text.

Adjective	Noun	Adjective	Noun
famous	____________	angry	____________
happy	____________	important	____________
private	____________	public	____________

3 Complete the spaces in these sentences with words and expressions from the text. The first letter of each missing word has been given. The meaning of the word or expression is given in brackets.

1 She finds it difficult to c________ w________ bringing up two small children on her own. (deal successfully with a difficult situation)

2 When his wife was seriously ill, he decided to t________ some time o________ to look after her. (get permission not to go to work)

3 When I was young the Beatles were real h________ ; all the girls of my age thought they were wonderful. (attractive and famous men that women fall in love with)

4 The Government is clearly t________ b________ f________ the rise in unemployment in this country. (responsible for)

5 If w________ g________ r________ that Tom Cruise is staying at this hotel, there'll be hundreds of screaming fans outside, waiting for him to come out. (it becomes known by lots of people)

6 If they want to avoid scandals, people i________ t ________ p________ e________ have to be careful how they behave. (who are often in the newspapers or on TV)

Vocabulary

Wordlist on page 203 of the Coursebook

A Cinema and films

Use the clues below to help you complete the grid with words related to cinema and films. When you have all the answers you will find an extra item of vocabulary for number 11 down.

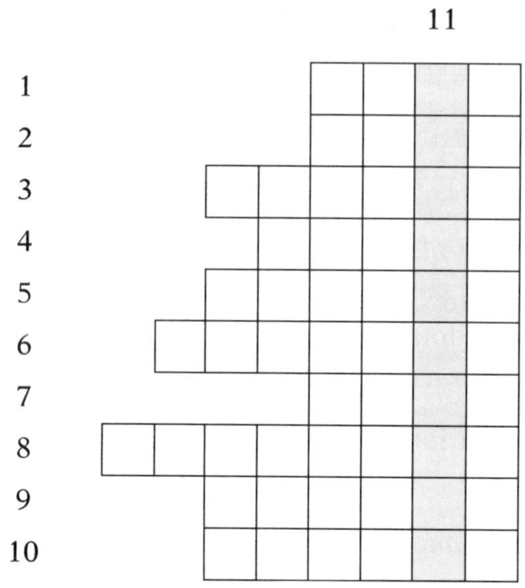

1 the people who act in a film
2 the story of a film
3 actors wear this, sometimes changing their appearance completely
4 a part of a film in which the action occurs in one place at one time, eg a love ________ , an action ________ .
5 a film which is intended to make you laugh
6 special ________ are unusual images or sounds created by using special techniques
7 another word for 'role'
8 a man who performs a dangerous piece of action in a film instead of the actor
9 a box _______ hit is a film which is very successful
10 a film that has a similar story and title to a film made earlier

B Expressions with *take*

Lexical phrase list on page 124 and Phrasal verb list on page 123

Complete the spaces with an appropriate word from the box. In **1–6** pay special attention to the prepostions in bold.

advice	risk	interest	notice	blame
courage	pity	care	offence	joke

1 He takes a very keen ____________ **in** music and often goes to concerts.
2 Don't say anything negative about her hair; she's very sensitive and might take ____________ **at** your remarks.
3 I was walking along a country road in the rain when a driver took ____________ **on** me and stopped to give me a lift.
4 If a team loses, it's normally the manager who takes the ____________ **for** the defeat and not the players.
5 Our neighbour has agreed to take ____________ **of** the dogs while we're on holiday.
6 The doctor told her to stop smoking, but she didn't take any ____________ **of** him. She still smokes 30 a day.
7 Although she really wanted to study archaeology, she took her parents' ____________ and went to law school.
8 Jamie likes making fun of other people but he can't take a ____________ himself. He gets so angry.
9 It took a lot of ____________ to ride his motorbike again after the accident.
10 She was taking a big ____________ when she changed career, but fortunately everything went well and she really likes her new job.

C Phrasal verbs with *take*

Complete each of the spaces with an appropriate particle.

1 She takes _______ her father; they're both as disorganised as each other.
2 I'd love to take ______ golf, but it's such an expensive sport.
3 We haven't really taken ______ the new boss; he's a little too formal for us.
4 Our maths teacher, Mrs Hill, is going to have a baby so Mr Bennett is taking ______ until she comes back.
5 They've taken ______ another receptionist at work; Alison couldn't manage on her own.
6 I had to stop going to yoga classes; they were taking ______ too much of my time.

Language focus

Grammar reference on pages 208 and 209 of the Coursebook

A Tenses

1 Complete each of the spaces with an appropriate past tense form of the verb in brackets. Choose from the past simple, past continuous, past perfect simple and past perfect continuous.

1 Susana ____________ (live) in Germany for three months when she ____________ (start) going out with Reiner. At that time he ____________ (train) to be a teacher and she ____________ (meet) him at a college disco.
2 When I ____________ (hear) about the motorway accident on the radio, I immediately ____________ (phone) my son to check that he ____________ (get) back safely. He ____________ (tell) me he ____________ (take) a different route home.
3 We ____________ (watch) a particularly romantic scene of a film at the cinema when my boyfriend's mobile phone ____________ (go) off. He ____________ (forget) to switch it off.
4 By the time we ____________ (get) to the party they ____________ (eat) all the food. In fact, it was so late that most of the guests ____________ (already/leave) and only two or three people ____________ (still/dance).

2 Complete the spaces in this story with the verbs in the box. Put the verbs in an appropriate past tense form.

go	hold	wait	tell	take	get
pass	sit	finish	drive	be	start

When I **(1)** ____________ my dad that I **(2)** ____________ all my exams, he **(3)** ____________ me to our local drive-through McDonalds to celebrate. While we **(4)** ____________ at the window for some more chips to be cooked, I **(5)** ____________ to the toilet inside the restaurant to wash my hands. Once I **(6)** ____________ , I rushed outside, jumped into the car and **(7)** ____________ eating the chips that my dad **(8)** ____________ in his hand. It was then that I heard an unfamiliar, and angry-sounding cough. I turned to discover that it wasn't my dad in the driving seat but a rather red-faced man; I **(9)** ____________ into the wrong car! My dad **(10)** _______ already ________ away from the window where they serve the food and he **(11)** ____________ in the car a short distance away, laughing at me. Needless to say, I didn't think it **(12)** ____________ very funny!

B *So* and *such*

Complete the second sentence so that it has a similar meaning to the first sentence, using the word given. **Do not change the word given.** You must use between two and five words.

1 We had such a lot of homework to do at the weekend!
so
We had ______________________________ to do at the weekend!

2 I thought there would be more people here.
so
I didn't think there would be ______________________________ here.

3 The food was so delicious that I couldn't stop eating.
such
It was ______________________________ I couldn't stop eating.

4 I enjoyed myself so much I didn't want to come home.
good
I had ______________________________ time I didn't want to come home.

5 It was such an interesting book that I stayed up all night to finish it.
so
I was ______________________________ that I stayed up all night to finish it.

C Linking words

In **1–6** underline the most suitable linking word or expression.

1 Last summer we stayed in an apartment near the beach *during/for/in* three weeks.
2 *As/During/Whereas* I was walking to school this morning, I found a £1 coin.
3 I looked everywhere for my glasses. *In the end/At the end/At last* I had to buy a new pair.
4 You're here *by the time/at the end/at last*! Where have you been? We were worried.
5 *Afterwards/After/After that* she'd taken the dog for a walk, she made a cup of tea.
6 'I saw the new Matt Damon film last night.' 'What did you do *afterwards/after/at last*?'

Use of English

FCE Part 5

Word formation: Adjectives ending in *-ing* and *-ed*

Use the word given in capitals at the end of each line to form a word that fits in the space in the same line.

The word you require may be an adjective or an adverb. It might be positive or negative.

1 *Scream* was probably the most ____________ film I've ever seen. **FRIGHT**
2 I get so ____________ when my dad starts singing. **EMBARRASS**
3 As the day of the exam approached, Karen became ____________ nervous. **INCREASE**
4 **a** I think I'll go straight to bed. It was a very ____________ journey. **TIRE**
b Yes, you must be ____________ . **EXHAUST**
5 I didn't really enjoy the film. The special effects were OK but the plot was rather dull and ____________ . **INTEREST**
6 Johnny Depp is not one of my favourite actors but he gave a ____________ good performance in *Sleepy Hollow*. **SURPRISE**
7 You look a little ____________ . Don't you understand what you have to do in this exercise? **CONFUSE**
8 It was quite ____________ to read so many negative reviews of the film. Critics wrote that the main characters were ____________ , but personally, I was very ____________ by the quality of the acting and would certainly recommend the film to other people. **ANNOY** **CONVINCE** **IMPRESS**

FCE Part 1

Multiple choice cloze

For questions **1–15**, read the text below and decide which answer **A**, **B**, **C** or **D** best fits each space. There is an example at the beginning **(0)**.

A lucky break

Actor Antonio Banderas is **(0)** ___*used*___ to breaking bones, and it always seems to happen when he's **(1)** __________ sport.

In the film *Play it to the Bone* he **(2)** __________ the part of a middleweight boxer alongside Woody Harrelson. **(3)** __________ the making of the film Harrelson **(4)** __________ complaining that the fight **(5)** __________ weren't very convincing, so one day he suggested that he and Banderas should have a fight for real. The Spanish actor wasn't **(6)** __________ on the idea at first, but he was **(7)** __________ persuaded by his co-star to put on his gloves and climb into the boxing ring. However, when he realized how seriously his **(8)** __________ was taking it all, he began to regret his decision to fight. And then in the third round, Harrelson hit Banderas **(9)** __________ hard in the face that he actually broke his nose. His wife, actress Melanie Griffith, was furious that he had been playing 'silly macho games'. 'She was right,' confesses Banderas, 'and I was a fool to **(10)** __________ a risk like that in the middle of a movie.'

He was **(11)** __________ of the time he broke his leg during a football match in his native Malaga. He had always **(12)** __________ of becoming a soccer star, of performing in front of a big crowd, but doctors told him his playing days were probably over. 'That's when I decided to take **(13)** __________ acting; I saw it as **(14)** __________ way of performing, and achieving recognition. What happened to me on that football **(15)** __________ was, you might say, my first lucky break.'

0	**A** familiar	**B** <u>used</u>	**C** normal	**D** annoyed
1	**A** practising	**B** making	**C** doing	**D** losing
2	**A** plays	**B** does	**C** gives	**D** fights
3	**A** When	**B** As	**C** While	**D** During
4	**A** kept	**B** continued	**C** carried	**D** insisted
5	**A** actions	**B** matches	**C** scenes	**D** stages
6	**A** interested	**B** keen	**C** enthusiastic	**D** happy
7	**A** lastly	**B** eventually	**C** at the end	**D** after
8	**A** competitor	**B** contender	**C** opponent	**D** participant
9	**A** very	**B** more	**C** such	**D** so
10	**A** take	**B** make	**C** have	**D** get
11	**A** remembered	**B** reminded	**C** recorded	**D** replayed
12	**A** hoped	**B** pretended	**C** dreamed	**D** looked forward
13	**A** up	**B** on	**C** to	**D** over
14	**A** further	**B** additional	**C** different	**D** another
15	**A** match	**B** pitch	**C** court	**D** course

Writing

FCE Part 2

Compositions: Advantages and disadvantages

1 **a** Read the following Writing Part 2 question and then follow the instructions in **b** below.

You have recently had a class discussion comparing films and books. Now your teacher has asked you to write a composition, giving your opinion on the following statement:

It is better to read a book than see a film version of the book.

Write your **composition** in **120–180** words.

b Read one student's plan and notes below and then the composition she wrote. As you read the composition put a tick (✓) next to those points in the notes which she decided to include in her answer. One of the points has already been ticked.

Composition
Book vs Film version

Plan

Paragraph 1	Introduction
Paragraph 2	Advantages of book and disadvantages of film version
Paragraph 3	Advantages of film and disadvantages of book
Paragraph 4	Conclusion

Advantages and Disadvantages

Book	Film
Advantages of book	**Advantages of film version**
can read anywhere and at any time	visual – makes story more memorable
good for mind – you use imagination ✓ interesting	can improve a story and make it more
can learn new words in your own language	special effects – all scenes in book are possible
more entertainment from a book – lasts long time	more elements in a film; music, colour, actors/actresses
can read a book many times	can see a film many times
Disadvantages of film	**Disadvantages of book**
film not always good interpretation	too much effort needed
too much violence	not everyone can read
film cuts and changes to story	

Nowadays, many people prefer going to cinema to reading the same story in a book. Both forms of entertainment have their advantages and disadvantages.

In the one hand, books help developing your imagination. You can decide what do the characters and places in the story looks like, whereas the film only gives you one interpretation, which may not be the best. Furthermore, the enjoyment from a book lasts more longer than from a film, and you can read it wherever and whenever you want. Another disadvantage of films is that they cut sometimes the most interested parts of the book, or change the story completely.

On the other hand, films are very visual, and this makes the story more memorable. Moreover, special effects are such good now that the most scenes of a book can to be shown on the screen. Besides this, some people prefer watching the film version because it takes less effort that reading.

On balance, I think always it is better to read the story first. After you can see it at the cinema if you want compare.

2 **a** Read the examiner's comments on the example composition and then follow the instructions in **b**.

Strong Points
This is clearly a well planned answer. The ideas are grouped logically into paragraphs and a number of linking words have been used to connect the different points. The composition is written in an appropriately formal style and there is a good range of vocabulary.

Weak Points
There are a number of grammatical errors throughout the composition.

b Read the student's composition again and correct the mistakes she has made. There are 15 mistakes altogether. Pay particular attention to the following areas of grammar:

- verb forms
- use of gerund and infinitive
- comparative forms
- position of frequency adverbs
- use of articles
- *so/such*
- adjectives ending in *-ing/-ed*
- prepositions

3 **a** Read the following Writing Part 2 question. Read the advice in **b** before you write your answer.

You have recently had a class discussion comparing video and the cinema. Now your teacher has asked you to write a composition, giving your opinion on the following statement:

It is better to watch a film at home on video than at the cinema.

Write your **composition** in **120–180** words.

b Before you write your answer make sure you plan what you are going to say first. You should:

- Write a paragraph plan giving a general idea of what you intend to include in each paragraph. Here is a possible plan:

Paragraph 1	Introduction: general statement
Paragraph 2	Advantages of video and disadvantages of cinema
Paragraph 3	Advantages of cinema and disadvantages of video
Paragraph 4	Conclusion

- Make a list of the advantages and disadvantages of watching films at home on video and at the cinema.

Advantages of video	Advantages of cinema
eg more comfortable watching a film at home	
Disadvantages of cinema	**Disadvantages of video**

- Decide which of these points you are going to include in your answer. Write your composition following your paragraph plan.

Don't forget!

- Connect your ideas using linking devices: page 35 in the Coursebook has a selection of these.
- Check your work for mistakes when you have written your composition: use the checklist in **2b** above.

5 Doing your Duty

Reading

FCE Part 1

Multiple matching

1 You are going to read a magazine article about an alternative type of school. Choose the most suitable heading from the list **A–H** for each part of the article. There is one extra heading which you do not need to use. There is an example at the beginning **(0)**.

A Advantages and disadvantages
B A calming influence
C Different from the rest
D Helping the slower students
E Creating the right environment
F A growing success
G Looking on the positive side
H Not what you would expect

The Little School of Calm

0 *H*

From the outside the Maharishi School in Lancashire looks extremely normal. Walk inside and you find rows of desks and children in uniform, just as you would do in many other schools. After a short while, however, you become aware of the wonderfully calm atmosphere and the extraordinary lack of noise in the building. Talk to the teachers and you learn that the school has no major discipline problems, there is no bullying and children are rarely absent. So what is the secret?

1 ______

Transcendental meditation and breathing exercises are an important part of the timetable at the Maharishi School. Pupils are taught how to relax mentally by closing their eyes and silently repeating over and over again a 'mantra', or Word of Wisdom, at certain times of the day. Meditation is seen by some as an effective way of relieving stress, which teenagers experience in the form of exam nerves, bullying and family break-ups. Its supporters also say that it helps to overcome hyperactivity, anxiety and aggression.

2 ______

The school was started in 1986 by a group of parents who were dissatisfied with the state education system. The number of pupils at the school has increased since then from 14 to 100, with ages ranging from four to 16. Academic achievements are impressive and for the past five years pupils at the school have obtained the highest average GCSE exam marks for the whole of Lancashire. It's not surprising then, that more and more parents are sending their children to be taught there.

3 ______

Many people in the local community, however, are still unaware of the school's existence. Others view the school with suspicion and associate it with mystic cults or the hippy movement of the sixties. 'Local people don't really understand what goes on here,' explains one teacher. 'They just see us as a little strange and prefer to keep their distance.'

4 ______

Teachers from other schools, however, are beginning to take an interest in the methods of the school. 'After the silence of meditation the children are very aware, awake and receptive,' explains head teacher, David Yates. 'This is very beneficial for the teacher and means we have the best conditions for learning to take place. In some other schools teachers have difficulty just getting the students to listen. That is not a problem here.'

5 ______

If there is a child who is creating a problem, the school has a very thorough method of dealing with it. A four-page form has to be filled out by the teacher, but the first three pages of the form contain nothing but the child's good points. In this way the problem does not become the main focus of attention; parents and teachers are encouraged to consider the child's successes and achievements before they look at the last page.

6 ______

But what do the children who study there think of the school's approach? 'Meditation really helps me with my work,' says 15-year-old Ruth. 'It makes me relaxed and I don't get nervous during exams. It's a shame it's such a small school, though. I can't study music because there aren't enough pupils, and when we read plays by Shakespeare we all have to read three or four parts each. But I love it here, and I know I'll miss the peace and quiet when I have to leave.'

2 **a** Complete each space in the table with the corresponding adjective or noun from the text. The numbers in brackets refer to the paragraphs in which the words appear.

Adjective	Noun
1 ____________ (0)	absence
2 wise	____________ (1)
3 anxious	____________ (1)
4 aggressive	____________ (1)
5 ____________ (2)	dissatisfaction
6 suspicious	____________ (3)
7 distant	____________ (3)
8 difficult	____________ (4)
9 ____________ (4)	benefit
10 ____________ (6)	nerve

b Complete each of the spaces with a word from the table.

1 Chris has been ____________ from school for three days. I hope it's nothing serious.

2 The main reason for his ____________ with the job is the low salary.

3 Police officers became ____________ of a shabbily-dressed man carrying a sports bag.

4 I shall always remember my grandfather as a man of great knowledge and ____________ .

5 Examinations are often the cause of great ____________ , particularly for nervous children.

6 They say that a glass of wine a day is ____________ to your health, but I don't see how alcohol can be good for you.

3 There are several expressions in English with two words joined by 'and'. Here is an example from the text:

Example: *I know I'll miss the* ***peace and quiet ...***

Complete each of the spaces with one of the expressions from the box.

law and order	up and down (= in both directions)
black and white	now and again (= occasionally)
clean and tidy	here and there (= in various places

1 She ran ________________ the street, shouting for help.

2 My parents only had a ________________ television until recently.

3 And if you want to dance, there are a few night clubs ________________ .

4 The police are responsible for maintaining ________________ .

5 I go to the cinema ________________ , but not really very often.

6 I don't mind if you have a party, but you must leave the house ________________ afterwards.

Vocabulary

Wordlist on pages 203 and 204 of the Coursebook

A Jobs crossword

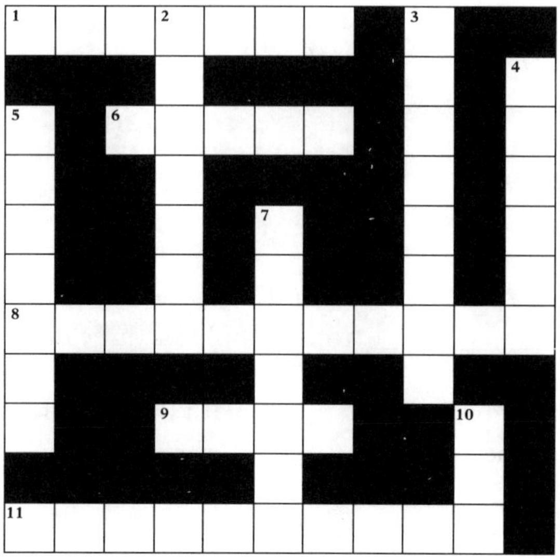

Across

This person ...

1 takes away people's rubbish
6 makes and sells bread and cakes
8 cuts people's hair
9 cooks in a restaurant or hotel
11 looks after the financial matters of a person or company

Down

This person ...

2 helps you to pass FCE
3 serves people with food and drink in a restaurant
4 gives advice to people about law and represents them in court
5 cuts up and sells meat
7 operates on people
10 treats sick or injured animals

B Questions and answers

1 Match a question in column **A** with an appropriate answer in column **B**.

A	B
1 Do you have a well-paid job?	**a** Yes, I have to make important decisions.
2 Is your job challenging?	**b** No, I have nothing to complain about.
3 Is it a responsible job?	**c** Yes, I have to treat everyone equally.
4 Do you have to be fair?	**d** No, I'll probably go on working.
5 Is fitness a requirement?	**e** Yes, I earn a good living.
6 Do you need artistic skills?	**f** No, physical strength isn't necessary.
7 Have you ever been on strike?	**g** Yes, it requires a great deal of hard work.
8 Will you retire when you're 65?	**h** No, it's not a particularly creative job.

2 Which of the following jobs might the person being interviewed in exercise 1 have? More than one answer may be possible.

firefighter	cook	judge	accountant	police officer
civil servant	surgeon	politician	architect	company director

C Expressions with *work*

In **1–7** below write the correct form of the verb *work* in the first space and one of the words or expressions from the box in the second space.

full-time	long hours	overtime	for myself
flexitime	part-time	my way up	shifts

1 I __________ ten hours __________ last week and earned £150 on top of my normal salary.

2 I've always __________ __________ ; I couldn't imagine not being my own boss.

3 You should be prepared __________ __________ as an accountant; eight in the morning till eight in the evening is not uncommon.

4 I'm __________ __________ at the moment; four hours instead of the normal eight. I'll probably go back to __________ __________ when John's old enough to go to school.

5 I'd quite like __________ __________ ; if you oversleep your boss doesn't get angry, and if you want to leave work early, you can.

6 My husband's a police officer so he __________ __________ . He prefers working nights; that way he gets to see more of the kids.

7 I've succeeded in __________ __________ to the top of this company; from messenger boy to managing director in 15 years.

Language focus

Grammar reference on pages 209 and 210 of the Coursebook

Obligation, necessity and permission

1 Complete the spaces with the correct form of one of the following verbs. In some cases more than one answer may be possible.

must	have to	need to	should

1 I know it's not my business, but if you're not feeling very well, then I think you __________ take the day off work.

2 We were planning to go out tonight but I __________ finish writing this report for my boss instead.

3 If you feel you __________ look up any words in the text, use an English–English dictionary.

4 I __________ remember to get some eggs on the way home from work tonight. I want to make a cake.

5 __________ write a story about ourselves or can we write one about someone we know?

6 I'm sorry I'm a bit late – I __________ go to a meeting and it lasted longer than I expected.

7 I've told you before, you __________ hand in your homework to me on time – I don't want __________ tell you again!

8 You really __________ try and stop biting your nails. They look so ugly like that.

2 For questions **1–8** decide which answer **A**, **B** or **C** best fits each space.

1 You __________ take an umbrella; it's not going to rain.
A mustn't **B** can't **C** needn't

2 I think we __________ to phone Marta and ask her if she wants to come.
A should **B** ought **C** can

3 The best thing about my job is that I ____________ to get up early. I don't start until 10 a.m.
A needn't **B** don't have **C** am not supposed

4 A 'Non-uniform Day' is a day when we're ____________ to wear normal clothes to school if we want.
A let **B** made **C** allowed

5 We'd ____________ make too much noise; we might wake the baby up.
A better not **B** shouldn't **C** ought not to

6 Where have you been? You were ____________ to be here half an hour ago!
A allowed **B** supposed **C** had

7 The rules are very clear. You know you ____________ jewellery to school.
A mustn't **B** don't have to **C** don't need to

8 I ____________ to stay at my friend's house last night.
A may **B** could **C** was allowed to

3 Complete the two spaces in each sentence with the following pairs of words. The first one has been done for you.

needn't/must	shouldn't/must	can't/must	~~can/must~~	can/should	can/can't

1 **a:** Is it OK if I go to London with my friends at the weekend, mum?
b: You ___*can*___ go if you want to, but you ___*must*___ phone me when you get there.

2 **a:** Are you sure it's OK to come in here?
b: Well, we ____________ really be here, but I ____________ just show you this.

3 **a:** Could I borrow an atlas?
b: Well, you ____________ certainly have a look at it here, but you ____________ take it home with you, I'm afraid.

4 **a:** Do I have to write the date on this piece of work?
b: No, you ____________ write the date, but you ____________ remember to put your name.

5 **a:** Could I take the dog for a walk?
b: Yes, of course you ____________ , but I think you ____________ wear your boots, don't you? It's very wet outside.

6 **a:** My parents won't let me go and see that film.
b: Well, if you ____________ see it now, you ____________ try and see it when you're older.

Use of English

FCE Part 3

Transformations

Complete the second sentence so that it has a similar meaning to the first sentence, using the word given. **Do not change the word given**. You must use between two and five words, including the word given. There is an example at the beginning **(0)**.

0 It isn't necessary to bring your Coursebook to the class tomorrow.
need
You ___*don't need to bring*___ your Coursebook to the class tomorrow.

1 I'm glad smoking is prohibited on public transport.
allowed
I'm glad you ________________________ on public transport.

2 What's their expected time of arrival?
supposed
What time ______________________________ arrive?

3 I don't think you should drink any more coffee.
better
You ______________________________ any more coffee.

4 You shouldn't be so impatient.
ought
You ______________________________ patience.

5 I'm not allowed to stay out later than 10 o'clock.
let
My parents ______________________________ out later than 10 o'clock.

6 I always used to have to tidy my room on Saturday morning.
make
My parents always ______________________________ my room on Saturday morning.

7 The science teacher made me clean all the test tubes.
made
I ______________________________ all the test tubes by the science teacher.

FCE Part 5

Word formation

For questions **1–14**, read the text below. Use the word given in capitals at the end of each line to form a word that fits in the space in the same line. There is an example at the beginning **(0)**.

Don't forget!

You may need to use the negative form of an adjective or adverb.

A driving instructor

Susan Bird, 57, is a driving **(0)** _instructor_ in South London.	**INSTRUCT**
'I was working as a shop **(1)** ________________ and I realized I	**ASSIST**
wanted to do something more **(2)** ________________ . I saw an	**EXCITE**
(3) ________________ in the newspaper and I decided to apply.	**ADVERTISE**
That was over 20 years ago.	
You certainly need to have a great deal of **(4)** ________________	**PATIENT**
to do this job, as well as the **(5)** ________________ to repeat	**ABLE**
things several times without getting **(6)** ________________ .	**ANNOY**
Although they are sometimes accused of being bad drivers,	
women tend to drive more **(7)** ________________ than men and	**CARE**
they don't mind **(8)** ________________ told what to do. Men, on	**BE**
the other hand, usually have more **(9)** ________________ , but they	**CONFIDENT**
aren't very good listeners. Generally speaking, other drivers	
understand what it's like to be a **(10)** ________________ and are	**LEARN**
very considerate. **(11)** ________________ , however, some can be	
rather **(12)** ________________ ; I have been shouted at and insulted	**TOLERATE**
by **(13)** ________________ drivers who haven't been able to	**ANGER**
overtake. It's an extremely **(14)** ________________ job, though,	**SATISFY**
particularly when your students pass!'	

FCE Part 2

Open cloze

Complete each of the following spaces with **one** word. There is an example at the beginning **(0)**.

A new life

Throughout **(0)** _the_ nineteen nineties I worked **(1)** ________ an accountant in a large furniture factory in London. I had a responsible job and was earning **(2)** ________ good living. Unfortunately, **(3)** ________ company wasn't doing so well, and in 1999 I was **(4)** ________ redundant.

My husband and I **(5)** ________ always wanted to run **(6)** ________ own business, and we both felt that now was a good time to **(7)** ________ a risk and do something different. Jonathan, my husband, gave **(8)** ________ his well-paid but stressful job in the City and we bought a pub in **(9)** ________ village near York.

It took **(10)** ________ both quite a long time to **(11)** ________ used to living in the countryside. Everything happens **(12)** ________ a much slower pace here, but the people are friendlier **(13)** ________ in London and we couldn't imagine going back **(14)** ________ to live. We still work as hard **(15)** ________ we did before, but it's so much more satisfying working for yourself.

Writing

FCE Part 2

Short stories

1 Read the answer to the following Writing Part 2 task and then answer the questions below it.

You have decided to enter a short story competition. The competition rules say that the story must begin with the following words:

I was beginning to feel a little nervous.

Write your **story** for the competition in **120–180** words.

I was beginning to feel a little nervous. It was my first day at work. I said I could speak French but I couldn't. I hoped they wouldn't know that I couldn't. Everything went well. My boss was nice and he told me what I had to do. He introduced me to the other people. They were all very nice. I sat down at my desk and the phone rang. I took the phone and I started to panic. A woman was speaking to me in French and I couldn't understand her. The boss saw me. He took the phone from me. He spoke to the woman in English and then he started laughing. He told me it was his mother. She went to the dentist's and couldn't speak very well. She spoke to me in English not French!

Which of the following does the answer contain? Write Yes or No for each one.

a a variety of past tenses ______
b a wide range of vocabulary ______
c a selection of linking words ______
d logical paragraphs ______

2 Rewrite each of these four paragraphs following the instructions.

Paragraph 1
I was beginning to feel a little nervous. It was my first day **(1) at work**. I **(2) said** that I could speak French but **(3) I couldn't**. I hoped they wouldn't **(4) know** that I **(5) couldn't**.

Paragraph 2
Everything went well. My boss was very **(6) nice** and he **(7) told** me what I had to do. He introduced me to **(8) the other people**. They were all very **(9) nice**. I sat down at my desk and the phone rang.

Paragraph 3
I **(10) took the phone** and I started to panic. A woman was speaking to me in French and I couldn't understand **(11) her**. The boss saw **(12) me**. He took the phone from me.

Paragraph 4
He **(13) spoke to** the woman in English and then he **(14) started** laughing. He told me it was his mother. She **(15) went** to the dentist's and **(16) couldn't speak very well**. She **(17) spoke** to me in English not French!

Paragraph 1
Replace the words in **bold (1–5)** with a phrase from the box.

find out	had been lying	it wasn't true
as the personal assistant to a company director		
had claimed at the interview		

Paragraph 2
Replace the words and expressions in **bold (6–9)** with those given in box **a**:

a

friendly	explained to
helpful	my colleagues

and add the following linking words from box **b**, making any other changes which are necessary.

b

who	just as
at first	then

Paragraph 3
Replace the words and expressions in **bold (10–12)** with those given in box **a**:

a

a word she was saying	how upset I was
picked up the receiver	

and add the following linking word from box **b**, making any other changes which are necessary.

b

naturally	as soon as	when

Paragraph 4
Replace the words and expressions in **bold (13–17)** with those given in box **a**:

a

had just been to	burst out	answered
was having difficulty speaking properly		
had been talking		

and add the following linking words from box **b**, making any other changes which are necessary.

b

afterwards	to my surprise

3 Answer Yes or No again for the four questions in exercise 1, but this time about the paragraphs you have written.

4 Now write your own short story beginning with the same words.
Remember to include:
- a variety of past tenses
- a good range of vocabulary
- a selection of linking words
- logical paragraphs

Don't forget!
Don't forget to include the words in the question!

6 Relative relationships

Reading

FCE Part 3

Gapped text

1 You are going to read an article about a family. Seven paragraphs have been removed from the article. Choose from the paragraphs **A–H** the one which fits each space **(1–6)**. There is one extra paragraph which you do not need to use. There is an example at the beginning **(0)**.

Before you start

Read the 'How to go about it' box on page 55 of the Coursebook.

KEEPING IT IN THE FAMILY

For many people, the idea of being permanently surrounded by all their relatives may not sound like a very attractive arrangement. The occasional visit of an aunt and uncle, or a large family celebration at Christmas might be more acceptable.

0 H

This means that in the tiny Oxfordshire village of Cassington, the local driving instructor, car mechanic, plumber and doctor's receptionist all live side by side with their nearest and dearest. The houses even have interconnecting gates to allow easy access.

1 ______

'If there's an accident or the freezer breaks down, you know you can depend on your neighbours to get you out of trouble,' says Ian. And with more than 20 members of the same family in the same street, that's a lot of neighbours who are willing to help.

2 ______

Ian and his parents moved into the street 70 years ago, when Ian was just a small boy. Ian's father, James, who wanted to supplement his income as a farmer, decided to invest in property. When other cottages in the street became available, he bought them.

3 ______

When they eventually got married in 1948, Ian's father gave the couple one of the cottages. Most newly-weds at that time had to live with their parents, so they were delighted to have their own place. And that meant that three of the nine houses were already occupied by the same family.

4 ______

One of the last to join them was daughter, Yvonne, together with husband David and their children aged five and two. They had to wait two years before a cottage became available, but Yvonne is convinced it was worth waiting for.

5 ______

Inevitably, however, there are tensions, as with any family. 'Mum and I do sometimes have a row,' she admits, 'but never anything too serious. And if we do fall out, it's never for very long.'

6 ______

'In my lifetime there has not been a single divorce or break-up in the family. Sylvia and I have already celebrated our golden wedding anniversary, and we're certain there'll be many more such celebrations in Bell Lane in the years to come.'

A After that, other members of the family gradually came to live in the houses and by 1990 the Waters family occupied every house on the row. Cousins, brothers, sisters, nieces and daughters had all moved in.

B 'We're constantly going in and out of each others' houses,' says Ian Waters, grandfather of the family. Indeed, if there's a problem of any kind, help is always close at hand.

C Like Yvonne, Ian feels that there are far more benefits than drawbacks. He also believes that having one's relatives living nearby can help strengthen a marriage.

D 'One of the main disadvantages of living in the same street,' she adds, 'is the lack of privacy. You can't really do anything without someone else in the family knowing about it.'

E 'We have the perfect babysitting arrangement,' she says. 'If we want to go out, Mum and Dad don't have far to come. And if they can't make it, someone else always can.'

F Sylvia, Ian's wife, lived with her parents in a cottage just along the terrace from James Waters and his family. She first became interested in Ian when he offered to walk home with her one night after a dance.

G Ian Waters' family extends over three generations: the youngest is Samuel, the son of his wife's second cousin, aged 18 months; the oldest, Fred Watson, a cousin, is 99. But how did they all come to be in the same row of houses?

H But the Waters family is such a close-knit one that all its members live in a row of cottages next door to each other. The inhabitants of numbers 1–9 Bell Lane are all related.

2 How many words can you find in the text for different family members? Write the words in the table below.

Words for male relatives	Words for female relatives	Words for both male and female relatives
eg *nephew*	eg *sister-in-law*	eg *grandparent*
______	______	______
______	______	______
______	______	______
______	______	______
______	______	______
______	______	______

3 Homographs are words which have the same spelling but different meanings. They may also be pronounced in different ways. Here is an example from the text:

... all its members live in a ***row*** *of cottages ...* /rəʊ/ = line

'Mum and I do sometimes have a ***row****.'* /raʊ/ = argument

In **1–8** below, complete the spaces in **b** with a homograph of the word you need from **a**. Decide if the two words have the same pronunciation or not and tick the appropriate box.

	Pronunciation Same	Pronunciation Different
Example: **a** If there's a problem of any kind, help is always close at hand. **b** He's such a *kind* person; he'll do anything to help you.	✓	
1 a If there's a problem of any kind, help is always close at hand. **b** Could you ________ the window? It's a bit cold in here.		
2 a Yvonne and her family came to live in Bell Lane, too. **b** Shall we go somewhere else? It's ________ crowded here.		
3 a Most newly-weds at that time had to live with their parents. **b** I once went to see U2 play ________ in concert.		
4 a I'm sorry, but I don't really understand what you mean. **b** I don't think he's generous. On the contrary, he's very ________ .		
5 a There were two football matches on television last night! **b** I can't light the fire; I haven't got any ________ .		
6 a When I was a boy, I used to go fishing with my uncle. **b** I didn't have a pen, so I ________ a pencil instead.		
7 a I've just read a fascinating book about identical twins. **b** The restaurant gets busy, so you'll need to ________ a table.		
8 a The big wheel is the only ride I'll go on at the fair. **b** She's got lovely long ________ hair.		

Vocabulary

Wordlist on page 204 of the Coursebook

A Adjectives of personality

Match each of the adjectives to an appropriate description.

reserved	clumsy	fussy	dull	affectionate	ambitious	bossy	stubborn

1 She worries too much about detail. ______________
2 He's always telling people what to do. ______________
3 She keeps dropping things. ______________
4 He won't change his mind. ______________
5 She's a bit boring. ______________
6 You never know what he's thinking or feeling. ______________
7 She wants to get to the top of her profession. ______________
8 He never stops kissing his girlfriend. ______________

B Compound adjectives

Eyes which are the shape of almonds can be described as *almond-shaped*. A person who has very pale skin can be described as *pale-skinned*.
Both *almond-shaped* and *pale-skinned* are known as compound adjectives.
Singular forms of nouns are used, eg *finger-shaped biscuits, long-eared animals*.
What compound adjectives can be used to describe the following?

1 a man who has broad shoulders	a b ______-s ______	man
2 a woman who writes with her left hand	a l ______-h ______	woman
3 a girl whose hair is fair	a f ______-h ______	girl
4 a boy with a round face	a r ______-f ______	boy
5 earrings which are in the shape of hearts	______________	earrings
6 a girl whose eyes are brown	a ______________	girl
7 hair which comes down to the shoulders	______________	hair
8 a famous actor who people know very well	a ______________	actor

C Expressions with *have*

Lexical phrase list on page 124

Complete each of the spaces with one of the words from the box. Pay particular attention to the words in **bold** when making your choices.

difficulty	common	the strength	influence	sympathy	a go	an operation	a look

1 She'll probably have to have ______________ **on** her back.
2 Come and have ______________ **at** this insect.
3 I don't think I have ______________ **to lift** this table on my own.
4 I had ______________ **understanding** him; he spoke very fast.
5 My older brother had a big ______________ **on** me when I was growing up.
6 I've never been windsurfing, but I'd love to have ______________ **at** it.
7 It's a strange relationship; they don't seem to have anything **in** ______________ .
8 It's your own fault you've cut yourself; I have no ______________ **for** you.

Language focus

Grammar reference on pages 210 and 211 of the Coursebook

A Causative *have*

Write out the following sentences using the correct forms of causative *have* and the main verb. Add any other words which may be necessary.

0 I/have/coat/dry-clean/weekago.
I had my coat dry-cleaned a week ago.

1 We/have/car/repair/yesterday.
____

2 I want/have/photo/take.
____

3 She/never/have/ears/pierce/before.
____

4 I/have/hair/cut/5 o'clock/tomorrow.
____

5 They/probably/have/house/paint/next month.
____

6 I/always/have/my suits/make/Milan/now.
____

B Phrasal verbs

1 There are four types of phrasal verb.

1 Intransitive verbs Verbs not followed by a direct object.	eg *to grow up* Of course I know Portsmouth. That's where I **grew up**.
2 Transitive separable verbs The direct object can go before the particle (ie it separates the verb from the particle): or after the particle: The object pronoun can only go before the particle.	eg *to let someone down* You have **let** the whole school **down**. You have **let down** the whole school. You have **let** us **down**. (*not* You have let down us. ✗)
3 Transitive inseparable verbs The direct object can only go after the particle (ie it cannot separate the verb from the particle): The object pronoun can only go after the particle:	eg *to fall for someone* I **fell for** Gillian the moment I saw her. (*not* I fell Gillian for ✗) I **fell for** her. (*not* I fell her for ✗)
4 Transitive inseparable verb with two particles The same rules apply as for transitive inseparable verbs with one particle:	eg *to go out with someone* She wants to **go out with** Ewan. She wants to **go out with** him.

Deciding which type a verb is

In many dictionaries the position of *someone* (or *something*) in the infinitive will tell you if the verb is:

Separable		Inseparable
to let **someone** down (Type 2) ('someone' appears between the verb and the particle)	or	to fall for **someone** (Type 3) ('someone' appears after the particle) to go out with **someone** (Type 4)

2 The verbs in the following exercise all appear in the Phrasal verb list on pages 122 and 123.

One sentence in each of the following pairs contains a mistake which is related to the use of the phrasal verb. Rewrite the incorrect sentence to make it correct.

1 a I'm very fond of my grandmother. I've always looked her up to.
b My boyfriend was getting too serious so I decided to split up with him.

____

2 a I think I take my father after rather than my mother.
b We haven't really taken to the new history teacher; he's much stricter than Mr Hollis.

____

3 a Angela and Debbie have fallen out again; Angela borrowed Debbie's watch without asking.
b I don't earn a great deal but I get it by.

____

4 a I blame the parents. They haven't brought up him very well.
b Don't wear your baseball cap like that; put it on properly.

____

5 a We'll buy you a dog, but you must promise to look after him properly.
b He looked so lovely in the pet shop; I fell him for immediately.

____

6 a I've decided to take up swimming.
b These meetings take it up too much time.

____

C Relative clauses

Complete the spaces with appropriate relative pronouns, giving alternatives where more than one answer is possible. Add commas if they are required.

1 Mr Jones ________ has taught here for 15 years will be leaving the school at the end of term. He has accepted the post of head teacher at St Mary's, the school in ________ he began his teaching career in 1980.

2 a Yesterday I spoke to the boy ________ has just moved into the house on the corner.
b Do you mean the one ________ mum looks like Cher?

3 a Do you know a good place ________ we could go for a bop?
b Yes, we could go to that club ________ has just opened in Farndale Street.

4 The reason ________ we're going skiing in March is because it's much cheaper then. Obviously we'd prefer to go in January ________ the snow's better but we can't afford it.

5 The fox ________ is normally a very shy animal can often be seen in city centres. It tends to keep to residential areas ________ food is usually easy to find.

6 You're the only student ________ hasn't written a letter of application. What's more, it's the third piece of homework in a row ________ you haven't done.

7 I lost that necklace ________ I was wearing on Friday ________ made me very unpopular at home. It belonged to my eldest sister ________ boyfriend gave it to her for her birthday.

Use of English

FCE Part 1

Multiple choice cloze

For questions **1–15**, read the text below and decide which answer **A**, **B**, **C** or **D** best fits each space. There is an example at the beginning **(0)**.

Home-alone fathers

The number of **(0)** _*single*_ fathers has increased considerably in **(1)** __________ years in Britain. We spoke to one such dad, Steve Baker, about how he **(2)** __________ it all. Steve, 43, has **(3)** __________ up his two teenage sons since he and his wife **(4)** __________ up two years ago. 'It's no **(5)** ________ difficult for a man than it is for a woman,' says Steve. 'It's a full-time job, whoever you are. Fortunately for me, my employers were very **(6)** __________ in the first few months and they **(7)** __________ me take time off work to get myself organized.

As **(8)** ________ as the housework is concerned, I don't mind cooking, as I've always been **(9)** __________ at that; it's the ironing I can't **(10)** __________ ! Generally speaking, the boys and I get on very well **(11)** __________ but of course, sometimes we have rows. That's when I really **(12)** __________ having someone there with me to help me out. I have had a couple of **(13)** __________ in the last two years but they haven't worked out. That has a lot to **(14)** __________ with the fact that I put my kids before anyone **(15)** __________ . I take fatherhood very seriously.'

0	**A** alone	**B** only	**C** <u>single</u>	**D** unique
1	**A** recent	**B** nowadays	**C** last	**D** latest
2	**A** gets by	**B** copes with	**C** looks after	**D** takes care
3	**A** taken	**B** made	**C** grown	**D** brought
4	**A** divorced	**B** separated	**C** parted	**D** split
5	**A** very	**B** more	**C** much	**D** at all
6	**A** comprehensive	**B** understandable	**C** sympathetic	**D** supported
7	**A** allowed	**B** offered	**C** suggested	**D** let
8	**A** far	**B** well	**C** much	**D** soon
9	**A** well	**B** involved	**C** good	**D** interested
10	**A** support	**B** hate	**C** stand	**D** help
11	**A** each one	**B** each other	**C** one another	**D** together
12	**A** miss	**B** regret	**C** want	**D** need
13	**A** relatives	**B** relationships	**C** relations	**D** partnerships
14	**A** be	**B** do	**C** see	**D** go
15	**A** more	**B** other	**C** else	**D** besides

FCE Part 4

Error correction

Some of the lines in the following text are correct, and some have a word which should not be there. If a line is correct, put a tick (✓). If a line has a word which should not be there, write the word. There are two examples at the beginning (**0** and **00**)

The same but different

0 My brother and I are identical twins, but we're very different ✓
00 from each other. When we were younger than Paul was always *than*
1 getting into the trouble at school, and I never did anything wrong. ________
2 I was much more quieter and sensible and preferred staying at ________
3 home and being on my own whereas Paul who was very sociable ________
4 and went out a lot with his friends. We tended not to do very much ________
5 together when we were teenagers. He was far too much wild and ________
6 noisy for me and he probably didn't think I was enough interesting ________
7 to be with. Now that we're older, things have changed. I've ________
8 become more confident and enjoy going out and having had a good ________
9 time. Paul, on the other hand, has found out a girlfriend, who has ________
10 had a calming influence done on him. They're even thinking of ________
11 getting married, which it will please my parents; they've always ________
12 been a little bit worried about him and they'll be happy to see him ________
13 in a stable relationship at last. We get ourselves on better now than ________
14 we did it before, and although we live in different towns and therefore ________
15 don't see each other a great deal, we still keep in touch and often ________
speak on the phone.

Writing

FCE Part 2

Letter of application

1 Read the following Writing Part 2 task.

You have just read this advertisement.

Write your **letter of application** to Mrs Adams. Say why you think you would be suitable for the job and ask for more details about what you would be expected to do.
Do not write any addresses.

> **Summer holiday job opportunity**
>
> I am looking for a friendly young person for July and August to help look after my elderly mother while I go out to work during the day. As well as caring for my mother, you would be expected to perform light duties and do some cooking.
>
> Personal qualities are just as important as experience. Reasonable knowledge of English essential.
>
> Please write to Mrs Adams enclosing a reference.

2 The sentences on page 49 are from a letter which was written in reply to the advertisement in 1. Put them in the correct order and arrange them into paragraphs, according to the following paragraph plan.

1 Reason for writing ____________
2 Personal details and qualities ____________
3 Experience ____________
4 Questions ____________
5 Closing comments ____________

Dear Mrs Adams

a As well as being honest and reliable, I am always cheerful and can keep smiling in any situation.

b I am 16 years old and I go to school in Vilnius, the capital of Lithuania.

c You mention in the advertisement that I would have to carry out 'light duties'.

d I also have a great deal of patience, particularly when dealing with other people.

e I enclose a reference from my English teacher, who gives details of my level of English. I look forward to receiving your reply.

f I know I would enjoy helping your mother and I feel I have the necessary qualities for this job.

g I am writing to apply for the job you advertised in last month's issue of *Jobs UK*.

h Apart from my personal qualities, I have experience of looking after my own grandmother, who lives here at home with us.

i I would be grateful if you could tell me what these duties include, and how many meals a day I would have to cook.

j I help to wash her, go out for short walks with her and occasionally read to her.

Yours sincerely

Dalia Vaivadaite

3 Ending the letter

Underline the appropriate alternative in each sentence:

a When we give the name of the person we are writing to at the beginning of the letter (eg 'Dear Mrs Adams'), we put 'Yours *faithfully/sincerely*' at the end.

b When we write 'Dear Sir or Madam' at the beginning of the letter, we put 'Yours *faithfully/sincerely*' at the end.

4 Write an answer to the following Writing Part 2 task, using the paragraph plan and accompanying comments and questions to help you. You should write between **120–180** words.

Before you write

Read the information about Letters of application on pages 122 and 123 in Unit 5 of the Coursebook.

You have just seen the following advertisement in an English newspaper.

> We are looking for a lively young person to help look after our two children (aged eight and six) during the summer holidays. Applicants should enjoy being with children and be capable of keeping them occupied and entertained both inside and outside of the house. Reasonable command of English required. Please write to Mr and Mrs Jackson enclosing a recent photograph of yourself.

Write your **letter of application**.

Paragraph plan

1 Reason for writing

In which issue of which newspaper did you see the advertisement?

2 Personal details and qualities

- Mention your age, say what you do and give your level of English.
- Why are you interested in the job?
- What qualities do you have which might be appropriate? Select three or four adjectives from the Wordlist (Unit 6) on page 204 of the Coursebook.

3 Experience and relevant interests and skills

- What experience do you have of being with children?
- What interests and skills do you have which might be useful for this job?

Remember, you can invent information!

4 Closing comments

- What have you been asked to enclose?
- End in an appropriate way. Will you write *Yours sincerely* or *Yours faithfully*?

7 Value for Money

Reading

FCE Part 4

Multiple matching

1 You are going to read a magazine article in which four people are interviewed. For questions **1–15**, choose from the people **(A–D)**. The people may be chosen more than once. When more than one answer is required, these may be given in any order. There is an example at the beginning. **(0)**

Before you write

Look again at the 'How to go about it' box on page 66 in Unit 6 of the Coursebook.

Which of the people state the following?

I don't have far to go to do the shopping.	0 *A*	
I have made unsuccessful complaints.	1	
I get on very well with the people below.	2	
I lived in the flat before I owned it.	3	
I don't very often have problems from noisy customers.	4	
I live in a busy area.	5	6
The character of the area has changed for the worse.	7	
The owner of the business took action to reduce the noise.	8	9
I used to have perfect working conditions.	10	
My sleep was often interrupted.	11	
I like the noise that normally comes from below.	12	13
I intend to go and live somewhere else.	14	15

'Just going downstairs to buy some cheese'

Living above a shop may be handy if you need something in a hurry, but it can also be a risky business. **Lynn Haywood** spoke to four people with a story to tell.

A **Masie Stigwall** I bought my flat in Chelsea with the money I made as a stunt woman in a Bond film. I've been here since the 1960s when I rented it from the friend of a friend. By the 70s I'd fallen in love with it and just had to have it for myself. It's in the King's Road, a bustling shopping street with fantastic amenities literally on the doorstep. I live above a supermarket, which was a nuisance at first; I was regularly woken up by people stacking shelves at night, and then, of course, there were the early morning deliveries. However, the owners were very reasonable when I complained and they sound-proofed the ceiling, which helped cut down the noise.

B **Paul Burton** When I first moved here I had the peace and quiet I needed to write the novel I was working on. The shop below sold wool and knitting accessories and there was a butcher's, a baker's and one or two other specialist shops in the street. They've all gone now, unfortunately; they couldn't compete with the out-of-town shopping malls and supermarkets which were springing up everywhere. The wool shop turned into a hairdresser's and now you wouldn't believe what I have to put up with. If it isn't loud music, it's the television at full volume, and then there's everyone shouting above the noise of the hairdryers. I've had words with them on more than one occasion, but they just ignore me.

C **Judie Marland** Everyone thinks that living above a pub must be a nightmare. I've been lucky, though; the landlord of the pub is very considerate and, apart from the occasional drunk singing outside at midnight, so are the people who drink there. A few years ago the landlord and I came to an agreement that he wouldn't play music above a certain volume after 10 o'clock. After a while he decided to cut out music altogether, and all I hear now is a gentle hum of conversation coming up through the floor, which I find very relaxing. I'll be sad to leave the place, but I've got my eye on a large detached house in a village near here. It's the space I need.

D **Arthur Short** It's the smell which has forced us to put our flat up for sale. Fish and chip shops are, by their nature, very smelly and there is no way we or the owner can do anything about it, so there's no point complaining. In fact, I'm on first-name terms with everyone down there and I often pop in to say hello. The noise isn't a problem; this is a lively part of town and we've always preferred places where we can hear people coming and going. We wouldn't have it any other way. We're moving out because we're tired of friends holding their nose every time they speak to us. It's getting beyond a joke now.

2 Match each phrasal verb **(1–6)** to its meaning **(a–f)** as it is used in the text. The letter in brackets indicates the paragraph in which the phrasal verb appears.

1 cut down (A)	**a** stop (playing/doing/eating etc)
2 spring up (B)	**b** tolerate
3 turn into (B)	**c** stop living in a house/flat
4 put up with (B)	**d** reduce
5 cut out (C)	**e** become (something different)
6 move out (D)	**f** appear suddenly

3 Complete each of the spaces with the correct form of an appropriate phrasal verb from exercise 2.

1 There were clear blue skies at first, but then it ____________ a really horrible day.
2 It's so noisy here; I don't know how you ____________ it.
3 They had a big row, after which Jim ____________ and went to live with his mother.
4 A few years ago no one here knew what a cybercafe was; now they're ____________ all over the city.
5 The doctor says he should ____________ on the amount of whisky he drinks, but he doesn't have to ____________ alcohol altogether.

4 Find expressions in the texts which have the following meanings. The letters in brackets refer to the relevant paragraphs.

1 I've complained to them (B) ____________
2 made a decision together (C) ____________
3 I'm interested in buying (C) ____________
4 advertise that we want to sell (D) ____________
5 I'm friendly with (D) ____________
6 it's becoming irritating (D) ____________

Vocabulary

Wordlist on page 204 of the Coursebook

A Wordsearch

Find 14 words related to shopping in the wordsearch and write them in the spaces given below. There are seven shopkeepers and seven things you find in a shop or a supermarket. The words go forwards or backwards, up or down, or diagonally.

T	T	T	S	I	R	O	L	F	G
F	R	T	I	I	E	A	E	R	C
R	O	N	G	L	L	A	O	G	H
E	L	E	O	F	L	C	E	R	E
T	L	G	O	I	E	H	L	E	C
N	E	A	D	R	W	E	S	H	K
U	Y	S	S	S	E	C	I	C	O
O	H	W	A	H	J	K	A	T	U
C	H	E	M	I	S	T	A	U	T
C	N	N	I	A	G	R	A	B	T

1 ____________ **8** ____________
2 ____________ **9** ____________
3 ____________ **10** ____________
4 ____________ **11** ____________
5 ____________ **12** ____________
6 ____________ **13** ____________
7 ____________ **14** ____________

B Multiple choice

In sentences **1–10** decide which answer, **A**, **B**, **C** or **D**, best fits each space.

1 If you decide you don't like it, bring it back and we'll give you a ________ .
A receipt **B** refund **C** guarantee **D** reward

2 I'm sorry, we don't have any in stock at the moment, but they are on ________ .
A request **B** demand **C** order **D** ask

3 Have you been to the new shopping centre on the ________ of town?
A centre **B** middle **C** outskirts **D** suburbs

4 They didn't have any ________ peas; only tinned or frozen.
A fresh **B** convenient **C** new **D** recent

5 If it's not working, take it back to the shop. They have to replace ________ goods by law.
A mistaken **B** faulty **C** lazy **D** incorrect

6 Do you like my new dress? I bought it in the January ________ .
A offers **B** reductions **C** bargains **D** sales

7 I only got the cheese because it was on ________ ; it was £5 a kilo instead of £7.
A offer **B** reduction **C** bargain **D** sales

8 It says £5.60 on the label. You've ________ me £6.50.
A taken **B** deducted **C** reduced **D** charged

9 I have to buy Doggy Chunks for Fifi; she won't eat any other ________ of dog food.
A selection **B** brand **C** mark **D** variation

10 This car was the most expensive purchase I've ever ________ .
A made **B** taken **C** put **D** done

C Phrasal verbs with *come*

Phrasal verb list on page 122

Complete the spaces with an appropriate particle.

1. John's just phoned to say he can't come tonight; he's come ________ with a bad cold.
2. If you come ________ my red pen when you're tidying up, could you let me have it?
3. I was talking to the boss this morning and the subject of my promotion came ________ in the conversation.
4. My mum said she'd come ________ with a brilliant idea for saving money; then she said she was going to reduce my pocket money!
5. Some friends of ours came ________ last night and we watched the basketball on telly.

D Expressions with *come*

Lexical phrase list on page 125

Replace the underlined part in each sentence below with an expression from the box which has the same meaning.

come to terms with	come on	come into fashion
come in handy	come true	come to

1. We've just bought my gran a mobile phone. It might <u>be useful</u> if she has an accident or something.
2. 'Oh, <u>hurry up</u>, Sandra. We're going to be late!'
3. I never thought flared trousers would <u>become popular</u> again.
4. After the injury he found it difficult to <u>accept and deal with</u> the fact that he would never again play football professionally.
5. Winning the lottery was like a dream <u>which had become a reality</u> for us.
6. 'I bought a blouse, a skirt and a pair of shoes.'
'How much did that <u>cost</u> altogether?'

E Word formation: Nouns

Noun forms for the following verbs can be found in the reading text on page 84 in Unit 7 of the Coursebook. Fill in the table and then complete the spaces in the exercise below with words from the table.

Verb	Noun	Verb	Noun
1 try	___________	**6** announce	___________
2 cure	___________	**7** behave	___________
3 like	___________	**8** create	___________
4 split	___________	**9** assist	___________
5 consult	___________	**10** appear	___________

a He has a ___________ for good whisky, and he makes special trips to Scotland to buy it.
b I'd like to make a little ___________ ; Shelley and I have decided to get married.
c I have a six-month ___________ period and if they like the way I work, they'll give me a permanent contract.
d Her parents are worried about her ___________ at school. She's always getting into trouble.
e The opening of a new car factory in Oxford has led to the ___________ of 2,000 new jobs.

Language focus

Grammar reference on pages 211 and 212 of the Coursebook

A Contrasting ideas

Choose the most appropriate sentence endings. Sometimes more than one answer is possible.

1 I'm not keen on shopping for clothes, whereas
A my brother isn't either.
B my sister loves it.
C I'm not fond of shopping for food.

2 I often had rows with my brother.
A However, we sometimes fell out.
B However, we always remained good friends.
C However, we never hit each other.

3 I enjoy living in the town centre, despite
A the noise.
B it's so noisy.
C being so noisy.

4 Although we arrived late for the concert,
A we missed the first few songs.
B they wouldn't let us go in.
C we managed to get a good seat.

5 We got on well when we shared a flat, in spite
A of the difference in our ages.
B of her being much older than me.
C the fact I was much younger than her.

6 I'm glad I went to the sales, despite
A the long wait in the cold.
B of the fact the queue was so long.
C having to wait so long in the cold.

B The present perfect and past simple

For questions **1–15**, complete the spaces with the present perfect or past simple form of the verbs in brackets.

How things change!

The Office for National Statistics **(1)** ____________________ (just/publish) a book which records how life in Britain **(2)** ____________________ (change) since the beginning of the 20th century.
Over the last 100 years or so, life expectancy **(3)** ____________________ (increase) dramatically. In 1901 men generally **(4)** ____________________ (expect) to live to 45, while women **(5)** ____________________ (live) four years longer. Since then the figure **(6)** ____________________ (rise) to 74 and 79 respectively and the number of people aged over 50 **(7)** ____________________ (double) from one sixth to one third of the population.
There **(8)** ____________________ (be) changes, too, in the types of illness that people suffer from. Smallpox and diphtheria **(9)** ____________________ (disappear) in Britain many years ago whereas cancer, AIDS and heart disease are now predominant.
In the last 30 years the nation **(10)** ____________________ (become) wealthier: in the early 1970s the average weekly wage **(11)** ____________________ (be) £160; now it is twice that figure at over £340. One of the most significant changes **(12)** ____________________ (take) place in the area of car ownership. The motor car **(13)** ____________________ (have) its first test in Britain in 1896; by 1950 there **(14)** ____________________ (be) two million cars on the roads, and in 1998 this figure **(15)** ____________________ (stand) at 22 million.

C Correcting mistakes

Find the mistakes in the following sentences and rewrite them so that they are correct.

1 My father's been worked as a shop assistant for over 15 years.

____

2 I've been breaking my leg three times in the last few years.

____

3 Charlie Chaplin has been one of the greatest comic actors of the silent movies.

____

4 Do you realize how long time I've been waiting here for you?

____

5 This is the first time I see this film.

____

6 James and I have known each other since many years.

____

7 It's over two years since I play football.

____

8 I cleaned three rooms of the house so far today; I'll do the other two this afternoon.

____

Use of English

FCE Part 3

Transformations

Complete the second sentence so that it has a similar meaning to the first sentence, using the word given. **Do not change the word given**. You must use between two and five words, including the word given. There is an example at the beginning **(0)**.

0 I wasn't surprised to hear that he'd failed.
no
It came ___*as no surprise*___ to me to hear that he'd failed.

1 They haven't decided whether to sack him or not.
come
They haven't ______________________ about whether to sack him or not.

2 Peter has gone on a sailing course in spite of being unable to swim.
although
Peter has gone on a sailing course ______________________ to swim.

3 Although the train was late, we managed to get there on time.
despite
We managed to get there on time, ______________________ late.

4 I'd rather walk than catch a bus.
rather
I'd prefer ______________________ a bus.

5 I'd prefer to leave later if you don't mind.
yet
I'd rather ______________________ if you don't mind.

6 He started to learn French six years ago.
learning
He ______________________ six years.

7 We haven't seen each other for ten years.
last
The ______________________ each other was ten years ago.

FCE Part 5

Word formation

Use the word given in capitals at the end of each line to form a word that fits in the space in the same line. There is an example at the beginning **(0)**.

Village life

In 1997, tired of the noise and **(0)** *pollution* of the city, best-selling	**POLLUTE**
author Will Smith and his family moved out to Chersey, a	
(1) ____________ village in the Suffolk countryside, with 53	**PICTURE**
(2) ____________ and one shop. Three years later they sold their	**INHABIT**
(3) ____________ 16th century cottage and moved back to London,	**BEAUTY**
where they now live in a smart new **(4)** ____________ on the outskirts	**NEIGHBOUR**
of the city. So what happened? 'Chersey seemed an idyllic place	
to live,' explains Will, 'a quiet, **(5)** ____________ old village in extremely	**PEACE**
(6) ____________ surroundings. However, we soon became aware of	**PLEASE**
the **(7)** ____________ of village life. With so little to do in Chersey, and	**ADVANTAGE**
because the buses were so **(8)** ____________ , our teenage children	**FREQUENT**
became **(9)** ____________ on us to take them everywhere in the car.	**DEPEND**
As for our own social life, the neighbours were rather cold and	
(10) ____________ , so we felt very isolated and lonely. It was not	**FRIEND**
the rural idyll we had expected.'	

FCE Part 2

Open cloze

Complete each of the following spaces with **one** word. There is an example at the beginning **(0)**.

On-line shopping

On-line shopping is (0) *one* of the fastest growing areas of the Net, offering users **(1)** ____________ large number of advantages over conventional shopping. Customers have access **(2)** ____________ a wider range of goods **(3)** ____________ in any shopping centre; **(4)** ____________ are no queues or parking problems; 'shops' are open 24 hours **(5)** ____________ day and purchases **(6)** ____________ delivered to your door. What's **(7)** ____________ , prices are competitive, and on-line price comparison services enable you to find **(8)** ____________ best bargains. These sites search the Net **(9)** ____________ a product and then show you **(10)** ____________ much different on-line stores are charging. Once you have decided **(11)** ____________ you are going to buy, and who you are going to buy it from, simply click **(12)** ____________ the 'add to shopping basket' icon. **(13)** ____________ you change your mind later and decide **(14)** ____________ to make the purchase, you can always cancel your order. Select the 'proceed to checkout' icon when you have everything you want, give your payment details and wait for delivery, **(15)** ____________ may take only a few days.

Writing

FCE Part 2

Descriptions

Read the following Writing Part 2 instructions.

You have just seen the following advertisement:

ALPHA CAMERAS

5th Annual Writing Competition

PEOPLE AND PLACES

For this year's competition we'd like you to write about a photograph which has both people you know and one or more buildings in it. Describe what the picture shows and tell us what memories it brings back to you.

The three best entries will each win an Alpha Beta X1 digital camera.

Write your **description** for the writing competition in **120–180** words.

A Structure

Read the model answer and decide which of these two paragraph plans it follows.

A	B
1 Introduction: general description of photo **2** Description of people and memories they bring back **3** Description of buildings and memories they bring back **4** Conclusion: final comments	**1** Introduction: general description of photo **2** Description of people and buildings **3** Memories which the photograph brings back **4** Conclusion: final comments

The picture shows me at the age of eight, standing with my brothers in front of a long row of terraced houses which are all identical and all the same dull grey colour. This is where I grew up, in a rather run-down area on the outskirts of Birmingham.

Despite the monotonous and fairly depressing surroundings, we're all smiling cheerfully, which reminds me of how happy our family was. We look extremely filthy and I remember how we all used to play football in the muddy field opposite our house.

We lived next to a huge industrial estate and in the background you can see several very tall chimneys with thick black smoke pouring out of them. I'll never forget my father setting off on his bicycle every morning to go to work in one of the factories to which the chimneys belonged. He would always play with us when he came home in the evening.

He retired last year, but I work there now in an office and I keep this framed photograph on my desk.

B Language analysis

a Read the model again and find examples of the following:

Types of buildings and parts of a town:
row of terraced houses

Adjectives to describe buildings and parts of a town:
identical

Adjectives to describe people:
happy

b Now answer the following questions about the model:

Which words are used to modify adjectives?
very (tall)

Which words and expressions are used to introduce memories?
which reminds me of ...

Which verb forms are used to talk about regular events in the past?

Which phrasal verbs have been used?

C Planning

Now plan your own entry for the competition, following these steps:

1 Decide which photograph you are going to write about.
Remember, it may be real or invented, but it must include people you know *and* one or more buildings.
The people can be friends, relatives, classmates, work colleagues etc.
The buildings can be old (eg a castle or a palace) or modern (eg a hotel or a skyscraper); they can be buildings you have visited regularly (eg your school or a library) or buildings you have only seen once (eg on holiday).

Don't forget!

Address both parts of the question: a description of the photograph **and** the memories it brings back to you.

2 Decide on a few adjectives you could use to describe:
- the people (see Wordlist for Unit 6 on page 204 of the Coursebook)
- the buildings and/or area (see Wordlist for Unit 7 on page 204 of the Coursebook)

Task: Look at the Wordlist for Unit 7 and find:
- three adjectives to describe old buildings
- three adjectives to describe buildings which are pleasant to look at
- three adjectives to describe big buildings

3 Write down three or four memories which the photograph brings back to you.

4 Choose the paragraph structure you are going to use: see A Structure.

Write your **competition entry.**

8 Time travel

Reading

FCE Part 2

Multiple choice

1 You are going to read a magazine article about round-the-world ballooning. For questions **1–7** choose the answer **A**, **B**, **C** or **D**, which you think fits best according to the text

Around the World in 19 days

On March 20th 1999, Bertrand Piccard and Brian Jones succeeded in meeting the world's last great aeronautical challenge by flying round the world in a hot-air balloon. It had taken them just 19 days. Gavin Sargent finds out how they did it.

Although the American newspaper publisher James Gordon Bennett first offered a prize for round-the-world ballooning in 1906, serious attempts to achieve this goal were only really made in the last decade of the century. Before Bertrand Piccard and Brian Jones successfully completed the challenge there had been 16 previous attempts, all of which had failed, some after travelling just 200 miles.

The technology required to make the flight is incredible. Piccard and Jones' balloon, the Orbiter 3, has two main components: the 55-metre high gas-filled envelope, and the capsule or 'gondola'. Most balloonists stand in a large basket but the capsules in round-the-world ballooning are more like the pressurized, computer-controlled cabin of a jumbo jet. Astonishingly for its size, it contains two beds and a small toilet divided from the main cabin by a curtain. You can just about stand up in it, and since it is so cramped, moving about is not easy. You can't leave it or sit on top of it for any length of time because you need extra oxygen at over 10,000 feet, and the Orbiter cruises at around 26,000 feet.

Controlling and steering the balloon is not easy, and all the pilots can do is change the balloon's height until they hit a wind blowing in the direction they want to go. These winds, called jet streams, are high above the Earth's surface and very unpredictable. A previous attempt by Virgin boss Richard Branson had started in Morocco in order to pick up the jet stream. However, Swiss watch manufacturers Breitling, having paid millions in sponsorship, insisted on Switzerland as the departure point for the Orbiter 3, despite Piccard's worry that this would add three or four days to the flight.

The Breitling attempt didn't get off to a great start. On the day of the launch, March 1st, the winds at the launch site at Chateau D'Oex were very high, causing the balloon to bump against the ground on take-off, damaging its video communications link with the ground crew. Once in the air, Piccard and Jones had to go west for three days before finding a wind that would carry them east on their route.

The flight, too, was not without crises. Piccard and Jones ran out of fresh supplies after five days and had to eat rehydrated food instead; by this time they were also dirty, smelly and exhausted. But the most dangerous part of the journey was the six days Piccard and Jones spent over the Pacific, where the size of the ocean meant they could not be rescued in the case of a forced landing. They also lost communications with their mission control for four days during this crucial period. When contact was eventually resumed they were sailing very close to the equator, where the winds were poor and their speed had slackened off considerably. The two pilots began to worry. The team's meteorologists told them to descend to catch the jet stream and, although a little nervous, they did as they were advised, and their speed started to increase.

The Orbiter 3 actually crossed the finishing line in the early hours on Saturday March 20th, but mission control wished to avoid a potentially dangerous night-time landing in the Mauritanian desert. Piccard and Jones were therefore instructed to head for Egypt. 'When we landed we were totally alone,' says Jones. 'After deflating the balloon we went to sleep in the gondola for two hours.' Eight hours after landing they were picked up by a military helicopter and taken to a small town called Mut.

The balloon was 'a bit of a mess', but the two men had finished a journey which, as the rules dictated, covered at least two thirds of the Earth's actual circumference, a distance of roughly 16,600 miles.

1 Attempts to fly around the world in a balloon
A began in 1906.
B have nearly all failed.
C were all made in the 1990s.
D all lasted longer than 19 days.

2 What do we learn about conditions in the capsule of Orbiter 3?
A The pilots found it difficult to sleep.
B The pilots had to wear oxygen masks.
C There was no fresh food.
D There was little room.

3 In order to change the direction of the balloon, the pilots
A fly very high above the Earth's surface.
B try to predict the direction of the wind.
C use the computers in the capsule.
D search for the right winds.

4 What does 'this' in line 46 refer to?
A take-off from Switzerland
B Piccard's worry
C the Orbiter 3
D the jet stream

5 Orbiter 3 took off
A three days later than expected.
B in strong westerly winds.
C in difficult weather conditions.
D without important communications equipment.

6 Why did Piccard and Jones become anxious over the Pacific?
A They had lost contact with mission control.
B They were flying very high.
C They had slowed down.
D No one came to rescue them.

7 Why did the balloon land in Egypt?
A The pilots wanted to be alone for the landing.
B It was safer to land in daylight.
C It would have been difficult to find them in the desert.
D There was no one to meet them in Mauritania.

Don't forget!

Read the text through first for the general meaning, or gist, before you make your choices.

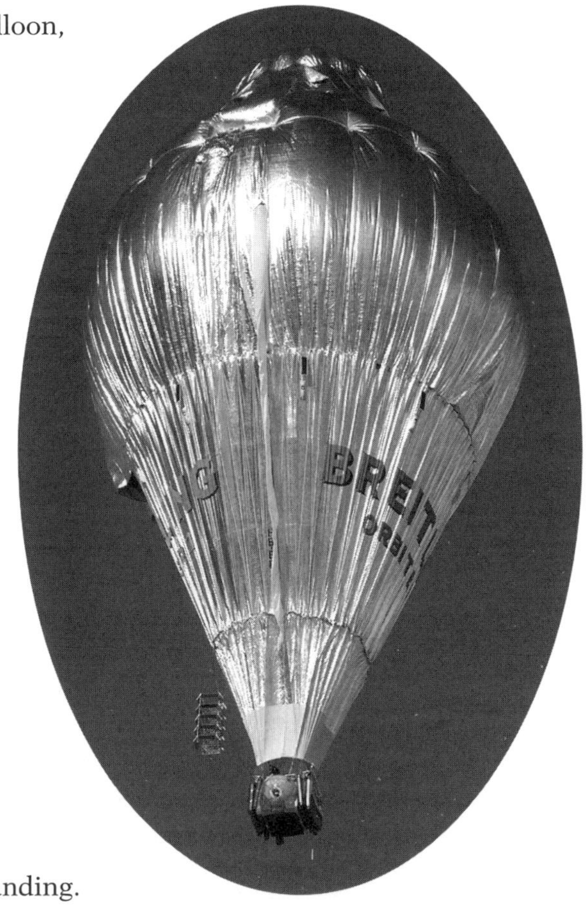

2 Find words or phrases in the article which mean the same as the words given below. The numbers in brackets refer to the paragraphs in which the words appear.

Example: a difficult thing to do ______ *challenge* ______ (Introduction)

1	succeed in getting (v)	______	(1)
2	parts (n)	______	(2)
3	small and with little space (adj)	______	(2)
4	travels at a continuous speed (v)	______	(2)
5	controlling the direction of (v)	______	(3)
6	take-off point (n)	______	(4)
7	hit against (v)	______	(4)
8	serious problems (n)	______	(5)
9	finished (v)	______	(5)
10	very tired (adj)	______	(5)
11	became slower (v)	______	(5)
12	collected (v)	______	(6)

Vocabulary

Wordlist on page 204 of the Coursebook

Confusing words

Choose the correct alternative in each sentence **1–10**.

1 Everyone thought the holiday was great *fun/funny* but I didn't have such a good time.
2 The area near the palace gates was *full/crowded* with tourists.
3 The facilities on this *camping/campsite* are excellent.
4 Have you decided where you're going on *holiday/holidays* yet?
5 We always *stay/live* in the same hotel when we go to London.
6 All the hotels at the ski *station/resort* are fully booked, unfortunately.
7 We didn't bring back any *souvenirs/memories* from our holiday. We didn't see anything worth buying.
8 From the top of the cathedral tower there are some spectacular *sights/sites/views* of the surrounding countryside.
9 The cost of the *trip/journey/travel* includes two nights in a four-star hotel with half-board.
10 She didn't enjoy the Mediterranean *voyage/cruise/tour* at all; she was seasick most of the time.

Language focus

Grammar reference on page 212 of the Coursebook

The future

1 Each of the underlined future forms is inappropriate. Rewrite each sentence with a more suitable future form.

1 Have you cut your finger? Come into the bathroom and <u>I put</u> a plaster on it.

____

2 Congratulations! I hear <u>you will have</u> a baby.

____

3 I've arranged to play tennis with Miguel tomorrow morning. <u>We're about to meet</u> at the sports centre at 10 am.

____

4 Can you wake me up before <u>you will leave</u> for work tomorrow morning?

____

5 I don't think <u>I'm getting</u> more than 50% in the exam; I never do well at physics.

____

6 This time tomorrow <u>we're going to sit</u> on the plane, probably somewhere over the Alps.

____

7 What <u>do you do</u> next weekend? Have you made any plans?

____

8 Phone me on Friday. <u>I'm speaking</u> to Greg by then, so I can tell you what his plans are.

____

2 Complete each of the spaces with an appropriate future form of the verb in brackets.

1 That bag looks very heavy. I ________________ (carry) it for you, if you want.

2 I ________________ (have) my eyes tested on Saturday. I've got an appointment for 10.30.

3 The autumn term ________________ (end) on December 23rd, the same day as my birthday. I ________________ (be) 15 then.

4 No, don't phone me at 8 o'clock. I ________________ (watch) the match at that time. Phone me at 9 instead; it ________________ (finish) by then.

5 I ________________ (get) some new clothes tomorrow; I've decided I need to change my look.

6 I think we should wait until Kevin ________________ (get) back.

7 Don't forget that when they get here this evening, they ________________ (travel) for over 12 hours, so I expect they ________________ (want) to go straight to bed.

8 'Katie? Hi, it's Antonio. Listen, I'm on the train at Croydon, so I ________________ (be) at Brighton station at five past nine. Can you pick me up?'

Use of English

FCE Part 3

Transformations: Phrasal verbs revision

Complete the second sentence so that it has a similar meaning to the first sentence, using the word given. **Do not change the word given.** You must use between two and five words, including the word given. There is an example at the beginning **(0)**.

Each of these transformations requires you to use a phrasal verb from Units 1–8.

0 I've had enough of your rudeness.
put
I am not going *to put up with* your rudeness any more.

1 I just can't wait for the Christmas holidays!
looking
I ________________________________ the Christmas holidays!

2 They'll probably employ him for two months in the summer.
likely
They ________________________________ on for two months in the summer.

3 The fact that bus travel is so cheap compensates for the lack of comfort.
makes
The low cost of travelling ________________________________ for the lack of comfort.

4 I think he's on the point of starting his own company.
set
I think he's about ________________________________ his own company.

5 Their relationship seems very good.
get
It looks as ________________________________ very well with each other.

6 Have you thought of a name for your dog yet?
come
Have you ________________________________ a name for your dog yet?

7 I'm not going to smoke ever again after today.
give
I've decided ________________________________ from tomorrow.

FCE Part 4

Error Correction

Some of the lines in the following text are correct, and some have a word which should not be there. If a line is correct, put a tick (✓). If a line has a word which should not be there, write the word. There are two examples at the beginning (**0** and **00**).

A holiday decision

0	This afternoon my wife and I are going into town for to get some	*for*
00	travel brochures so we can start thinking about our holiday this	✓
1	summer. We are normally agree about where to go each year but	______
2	this time we may be well have a few problems finding something	______
3	that it will satisfy both of us. Alice, my wife, has had a difficult	______
4	year at the work and she has already said to me that she wants	______
5	to relax herself for a couple of weeks in a Mediterranean resort,	______
6	sunbathing and sleeping as much as if possible. As for me, I'd	______
7	rather prefer do something more active than that; I know I'll	______
8	get by bored if we just sit on the beach all day getting sunburnt.	______
9	Yesterday a friend of mine showed me photographs of his holiday	______
10	last year and I must say it looked like very interesting. He and his	______
11	wife hired a caravan for four weeks and went on a tour of Ireland,	______
12	visiting different towns, sightseeing and sometimes go walking in	______
13	the countryside. The caravan was spacious and it equipped with	______
14	everything you need for a short touring holiday, including a shower.	______
15	I'll mention it to Alice later on; she is will likely to say no, but it's worth asking.	______

FCE Part 5

Word formation

Use the word given in capitals at the end of each sentence to form a word that fits in the space in the sentence.

1	As it grew hotter, even the managing director ______________ his tie and undid his collar button.	**LOOSE**
2	If we introduced another foreign language in the school, we'd have to ______________ the school day.	**LONG**
3	Owing to continuous heavy rain, driving conditions have ______________ in the past few hours.	**WORSE**
4	Don't come near me when I'm ______________ the knife, dear. I don't want you to cut yourself.	**SHARP**
5	Free divers are now diving to ______________ of over 80 metres.	**DEEP**
6	Then heat the sauce until it ______________ .	**THICK**
7	It's thought that listening to loud music on a regular basis can eventually lead to partial ______________ .	**DEAF**
8	His face had ______________ with anger. It looked as if he might explode!	**RED**
9	It was raining heavily in the morning, but by midday the weather had ______________ up and we were able to go out.	**BRIGHT**
10	There have been several serious accidents recently, so the police are ______________ up on drunken driving.	**TIGHT**

Writing

FCE Part 1

Transactional letters: Correcting information

Letters of complaint: pages 87–89 in Unit 7 of the Coursebook

Read the following Writing Part 1 question. You do not need to write an answer.

You have just read an entry for the town of Rington in a new guidebook of Britain. You know Rington very well and you disagree with many of the things which have been written.

Read the extract from the guidebook entry, together with your own comments. Then write to the publishers, telling them which points you disagree with **and** explaining briefly why you think people should visit Rington.

The Ultimate Guide Book – **Rington**

As you would expect, there are plenty of souvenir shops in the centre of Rington, selling a wide range of gifts from handicrafts to local honey. Unfortunately, the goods on sale are rather poorly made and tourists should think carefully before buying presents to take home. Unlike the souvenir shops, there do not seem to be enough places to eat in Rington. We recommend 'The Hungry Years' restaurant in Mossop Street for good English food, but be prepared for small portions and high prices. After lunch you might like to go for a walk alongside the River Bane, which flows through the town. The river will take you into open countryside, which, surprisingly, is just 15 minutes on foot from the centre. A pity the water is polluted, though. Rington is famous for its large number of historic monuments, many dating from Roman times. However, these are always crowded with tourists and long queues tend to form very quickly.

32

Comments:

- not all (→ "the goods on sale are rather poorly made")
- lots in Coney Street (→ "there do not seem to be enough places to eat")
- not any more (→ "A pity the water is polluted")
- max. 15 minutes' wait (→ "long queues tend to form very quickly")

Write a **letter** of between **120–180** words in an appropriate style. Do not write any addresses.

A Model

Read this answer to the Writing question on page 63, then complete each space with an appropriate expression from the box.

in addition, you claim your comment about	firstly, you say that no longer true	according to you fail to mention

Dear Sir

I am writing to complain about your new guidebook, *Around Britain*, which contains several inaccuracies in the entry for Rington.

(a) ______________ the souvenirs are poorly made. Although I agree this is sometimes true, I cannot understand why **(b)** ______________ the high quality handmade knives for which Rington is famous. **(c)** ______________ there is a lack of places to eat. However, Coney Street has a wide variety of cafes and restaurants, where tourists can have either a snack or a three-course meal.

Furthermore, **(d)** ______________ your guidebook, the River Bane is polluted, but this is **(e)** ______________. It has recently been cleaned and in some parts of the river it is possible to swim. I also disagree with **(f)** ______________ queuing for the monuments. These only become busy in August, when the longest that tourists have to wait is 15 minutes.

Rington is an attractive and friendly town, which offers tourists everything they need for a pleasant visit. I trust you will make the necessary corrections in the next edition of your guidebook.

Yours faithfully

Alice Matheson

B Analysis

Answer the following questions about the model letter.

1 Which linking words are used for contrasting ideas?

2 Which linking words and expressions are used for adding to the list of points?

3 Which words or expressions in the letter have the following meanings?

a incorrect statements ______________
b there are not enough ______________
c not correct any more ______________
d I hope ______________

C Adding relevant points

Candidates who write good answers to questions build on the information given by adding relevant points of their own. What extra information has the writer of the model added for each of the following? The first one has been done for you.

the souvenirs: *The high quality handmade knives for which Rington is famous.*

the restaurants: ______________________

the river: ______________________

the monuments: ______________________

D Writing task

Now write your own answer to the same question, but this time about the town of Blackingham described below. Read section 6 Preparation before you write your answer.

The Ultimate Guide Book – **Blackingham**

Visitors to Blackingham usually head straight for the historic centre, with its attractive Georgian architecture and 14th century cathedral. Traffic is a problem here, and the narrow streets quickly fill up with cars and lorries. This is inconvenient for both tourists and shoppers. Next to the cathedral is the famous Blackingham museum, with exhibits from the town's 2000-year history. Despite its reputation, the museum does not contain many interesting objects and visitors may be disappointed. After seeing the sights you might like to relax in one of Blackingham's two large parks. Both Victoria Park and East Hill Park are extremely pleasant with plenty of seats for you to rest your tired legs. However, younger members of your family may get bored as there is very little for them to do and see.

Blackingham is not known for its nightlife and now that the 'Gula Gula' discotheque has closed, there is nowhere to go dancing.

12

not any more

lots to see!

not true

yes, there is – 'Sherry's' and 'The Pink Panther'

E Preparation

a Adding relevant points of your own
Answer the following questions to give you some ideas.

the traffic:	What did the town council do to solve the traffic problem?
the museum:	What examples could you give of interesting things to see?
the parks:	What examples could you give of things to do?
the nightlife:	What type of music do they play at one or both of these discotheques?

b Answering the second part of the question
Write one sentence explaining why you think people should visit Blackingham. (See 'Adjectives for towns and villages' on page 204 in the Coursebook)

Write between **120–180** words.

Don't forget!

Use the words and expressions from the model letter.

9 Fact or fiction?

Reading

FCE Part 1

Multiple matching

1 You are going to read an article about Carnival. Choose the most suitable summary sentence from the list **A–H** for each part **(1–6)** of the article. There is one extra summary sentence which you do not need to use. There is an example at the beginning **(0)**.

A Part of the costume used to be worn to prevent recognition.
B The length of the Carnival period is not the same in all countries.
C The wearing of a costume is compulsory during the parade.
D Entrance to some parts of the Carnival is restricted.
E Carnival here grew from very small beginnings.
F Some of the Carnival traditions have not become quite so popular everywhere.
G Participants work together to win a contest.
H The tradition of Carnival has been adopted all over the world.

Carnival

0 *H*

Carnival was originally a Roman Catholic tradition which took place in the days before Lent, the period of 40 days before Easter. After spreading throughout Europe it was then introduced to other parts of the world, particularly South America and the Caribbean, where it was enthusiastically accepted by the native populations and then developed in different ways. Now it is a popular festival, uniting whole communities in dancing and other festivities, for days or even weeks on end.

1 ____

Indeed, whilst the Carnival season still normally reaches a high point in the days just before Lent, it may begin up to three months before. In Austria, where it is known as *Fasching*, the Carnival season officially starts on November 11th, whereas in New Orleans *Mardi Gras* opens on Twelfth Night, January 6th. London's own Notting Hill Carnival, imported by Caribbean immigrants in the 1950s, often takes place on two days in August, when about two million people fill the streets of West London.

2 ____

However, there is no Carnival celebration which rivals Rio for its spectacular parades, colourful costumes and the flamboyant nature of the people who take part. The main feature of the four-day event is the parade of the city's samba schools, which each consist of hundreds of people. The schools compete with each other in front of a huge number of spectators to give the best display of dancing and have the most elaborate costumes.

3 ____

There is also a competition in Venice, but the prize is awarded there for the most beautiful mask in the Carnival. Masks have long been an important part of *Carnevale*, originally to enable those who wore them to hide their identity while they behaved in a manner which was not entirely acceptable to contemporary society. The modern *Carnevale* is still theatrical, with many people wearing a costume, and of course a mask.

4 ____

Mardi Gras started up in New Orleans in 1827, but it is no less important or colourful than the 1,000-year-old *Carnevale*. The tradition was taken to New Orleans from Europe by a group of students who had been studying in Paris and who saw Carnival being celebrated there. Other young people took to the custom of dressing up and dancing in the streets and in 1837 the city organized its first parade, which in the early days had just one float. Now the parades are almost endless.

5 ____

In New Orleans anyone can take part in the big *Mardi Gras* street parade, but you have to belong to a 'krewe' if you want to get into one of the many balls which are held during the period just before *Mardi Gras*. 'Krewes' are special Carnival organizations, each of which has its own king and queen.

6 ____

But what of Britain's Carnival customs? Certainly, people mark the occasion: for centuries pancakes have been eaten on Shrove Tuesday, the day before the beginning of Lent. This was the traditional way of using up eggs and milk before a fast. But whilst Carnival parades can be seen throughout the country, the custom has never really caught on in the same way as it has in the capital. Perhaps British people are simply not used to extravagant or flamboyant behaviour.

2 Read the texts again, and find who or what the words in italics refer to. The paragraph numbers are given in brackets.

1 ... *it* was then introduced to other parts of the world ... (0)
2 ... *its* spectacular parades ... (2)
3 ... *which* each consist of hundreds of people. (2)
4 ... those who wore *them* ... (3)
5 ... while *they* behaved in a manner ... (3)
6 ... but *it* is no less important or colourful ... (4)
7 ... saw Carnival being celebrated *there*. (4)
8 ... each of *which* has *its* own king and queen. (5)
9 *This* was the traditional way of using up eggs and milk ... (6)

3 Match the verbs **1–6** from the article with the meanings **a–f** below. The paragraph numbers are given in brackets.

1 spread (0)
2 unite (0)
3 rival (2)
4 enable (3)
5 take to (4)
6 catch on (6)

a bring together
b start to like
c be as good as
d gradually cover an increasingly larger area
e become popular
f make it possible for

4 Fill each of the spaces with the appropriate form of one of the verbs in **3**.

1 The Internet __________ us to communicate with people on the other side of the world in seconds.
2 Although the first microwave was produced in 1955, they didn't __________ until the late 1960s.
3 The disaster has __________ the country and got everyone working together.
4 We bought my dad a computer for his 60th birthday, but he hasn't really __________ it.
5 The disease began in one region and then __________ throughout the rest of the country.
6 Video cassettes cannot __________ DVDs for their sound and picture quality.

Vocabulary

A Phrasal verbs

Phrasal verb list on page 122

Match each sentence beginning on the left with an appropriate ending on the right.

1 As soon as I **gave up**
2 The cooker was **giving off**
3 Suspected of **giving away**
4 He listened closely as they **gave out**
5 She said we had to **give in**
6 Street Aid is a charity which **gives out**
7 He says he can't **give back**

a **state secrets**, he was arrested and held in jail.
b **the homework** tomorrow morning.
c **smoking**, I felt a lot better.
d **food** to homeless people.
e **a strange smell,** so I got someone to look at it.
f **the money** I lent him until Friday.
g **the winning lottery numbers** on the news.

B Expressions with *give*

Lexical phrase list on page 124

Complete each of the spaces with one of the words in the box.

lift	example	idea	impression
call	party	hand	permission

1 'Risk' is a verb which takes the gerund. Can anyone give another ____________ ?
2 Dave gave me a ____________ to work in his new car this morning.
3 I can't move this table on my own. Can anyone give me a ____________ ?
4 The manager has given me ____________ to take two days off work.
5 He gave me the ____________ that he was bored; he kept sighing during the lesson.
6 I won't be at home tomorrow, but you can give me a ____________ on my mobile?
7 Would you give me some ____________ of what time you'll be coming home, so I'll know when to have dinner ready for.

C Collocations

One adjective in each group is not normally used in partnership with the noun in capital letters. Underline the word which does not fit. There is an example at the beginning **(0)**.

0 deep	impatient	<u>open-air</u>	loud	SIGH
1 piercing	loud	blank	high-pitched	SCREAM
2 tender	big	passionate	broad	KISS
3 full	precise	nervous	relevant	DETAILS
4 lengthy	piercing	impressive	boring	SPEECH
5 deep	tender	broad	friendly	SMILE
6 loud	full	nervous	cruel	LAUGH
7 impressive	nasty	great	terrible	SHOCK

D Revision: *get*

1 It was such a sad, depressing film; it really got me ____________ .
2 We all suffered from food poisoning on holiday. I'm OK now, but my mum and dad still haven't got ____________ it.
3 I'm going to try to get ____________ for the weekend. I'll probably go to the coast.
4 I don't know how they get ____________ ; they're both unemployed and they've got three children.

Language focus

Grammar reference on page 213 of the Coursebook

A Modal verbs of speculation

1 There is a mistake in five of the sentences in **1–10** below. Find the mistakes and rewrite the sentences to make them correct.

1 I can't find my keys. I think I might leave them on my desk at work.
2 The dog's barking a lot. He might be trying to tell us something.
3 Sally's not answering the phone. She can have gone away for the weekend, or perhaps she's just gone to the shops.
4 It's his birthday tomorrow, so he must be excited.
5 They said they'd found out what was wrong with the washing machine, but they can't have done because it's still not working properly.
6 **a:** Andrea never wears that blouse we bought her.
b: Well, she might not like the colour, it may not go with her skirts or it could not be the right size. Who knows?
7 Jim mustn't be going out with Sue; she's just got engaged to Doug.
8 It couldn't have run out of petrol. I filled it up this morning before we left.
9 It's a shame Mark hasn't come. He must decide to stay at home.
10 The tennis rackets aren't in the car. You must have forgotten to put them in.

2 Use modal verbs to give one or more explanations for the following situations.

Example:
He can't drive for two months.
He could have broken his leg or his wife might be using the car.

1 He looks exhausted.
____

2 She isn't eating very much at the moment.
____

3 There's a lot of traffic in the city centre today.
____

4 The plants have all died.
____

5 The police came to speak to the neighbours this morning.
____

6 John seems very happy these days.
____

7 Why are all those people shouting?
____

8 I was sure I'd parked my car here. Where is it?
____

B Question tags

Complete each of the following phrases with an appropriate question tag.

1 He hasn't been here long, ________________ ?
2 I'm getting old, ________________ ?
3 He plays for Barcelona, ________________ ?
4 You'd like to come, ________________ ?
5 She said she was ill, ________________ ?
6 Don't make too much noise, ________________ ?
7 Help me lift this box, ________________ ?
8 Let's go to the cinema, ________________ ?
9 Nothing serious happened, ________________ ?
10 No one lives here now, ________________ ?

Use of English

FCE Part 1

Multiple choice cloze

Read the text below and decide which answer **A**, **B**, **C** or **D** best fits each space. There is an example at the beginning **(0)**.

The wildman of China

Most people are **(0)** _familiar_ with the yeti, a large hairy man-like creature, which is **(1)** ______ to live in the Himalayas. **(2)** ______ , you might not have heard of the 'yeren' or 'wildman' of China, which was mentioned and drawn for the first **(3)** ______ more than 2,000 years ago. In the **(4)** ______ 40 years there have been over 200 **(5)** ______ of the yeren in the Shennongjia Nature Reserve in central Hubei province. **(6)** ______ the size of footprints which have been found, the yeren could weigh as **(7)** ______ as 300 kilos. Those who claim to have seen it have described it **(8)** ______ approximately 1.6 metres tall, with long red hair, rounded eyes and a broad forehead. It also seems **(9)** ______ of an incredible range of calls and noises. When disturbed, it is said to sound like a dog, a wolf, a donkey and **(10)** ______ a crying child.
In 1980 a Chinese scientist **(11)** ______ up in a gorilla costume and entered a forest in the **(12)** ______ of getting a closer look at a yeren. Not **(13)** ______ he failed, as have many others who have gone in **(14)** ______ of this elusive creature. Indeed, there have been **(15)** ______ many expeditions to find the yeren that the government has officially denied its existence, in order to prevent further damage being caused to delicate habitats in the nature reserve.

0	**A** aware	**B** conscious	**C** familiar	**D** known
1	**A** reported	**B** informed	**C** noticed	**D** announced
2	**A** Actually	**B** Instead	**C** However	**D** Moreover
3	**A** time	**B** event	**C** occasion	**D** moment
4	**A** latest	**B** ultimate	**C** recent	**D** last
5	**A** views	**B** visions	**C** sightings	**D** looks
6	**A** Taken	**B** Given	**C** Considered	**D** Seen
7	**A** much	**B** high	**C** far	**D** near
8	**A** like	**B** with	**C** as	**D** of
9	**A** able	**B** competent	**C** capable	**D** powerful
10	**A** just	**B** too	**C** well	**D** even
11	**A** wore	**B** dressed	**C** put	**D** changed
12	**A** attempt	**B** hope	**C** order	**D** wish
13	**A** especially	**B** hopefully	**C** surprisingly	**D** believably
14	**A** search	**B** look	**C** hunt	**D** sight
15	**A** too	**B** very	**C** so	**D** quite

FCE Part 5

Word formation

1 Write the adjectives and adverbs which are formed from the following nouns. Use the suffixes *-al*, *-ous* or *-y* and make any other changes which are necessary. There is an example at the beginning **(0)**.

Noun	Adjective	Adverb
0 noise	*noisy*	*noisily*
1 humour	______	______
2 ambition	______	______
3 benefit	______	______
4 hunger	______	______
5 anxiety	______	______
6 origin	______	______

2 Complete the table with the correct form of the words given. There is an example at the beginning **(0)**.

Verb	Noun	Adjective +	Adjective –
0 appreciate	*appreciation*	*appreciative*	*unappreciative*
1 ______	attraction	______	______
2 decide	______	______	______
3 excite	______	______	______
4 ______	imagination	______	______
5 ______	obedience	______	______
6 offend	______	______	______
7 please	______	______	______
8 ______	success	______	______
9 ______	thought	______	______
10 ______	tolerance	______	______

3 Complete each space with the appropriate form of the words in capitals. If the missing word is a **noun**, you may need a plural form. If the missing word is an **adjective** or **adverb**, you may need a negative form. There is an example at the beginning **(0)**.

0 He gave her a small present to show his *appreciation* for her kindness. **APPRECIATE**

1 I think it's an extremely ______ building; it's far too big and it ruins the character of the area **ATTRACTION**

2 I'm afraid I'm not very good at making ______ . I never know what the best thing to do is. **DECIDE**

3 There was a great deal of ______ excitement when the Queen arrived to open the new hospital. **EXCITE**

4 You really should read one of the Harry Potter books. They're very ______ written. **IMAGINATION**

5 He never does as he's told; he's so ______ . **OBEDIENCE**

6 You shouldn't take ______ . I'm sure he didn't mean what he said. **OFFEND**

7 I always have a glass of wine with my meal. It's one of my few ______ . **PLEASE**

8 78-year-old Bill Baxter has ______ completed his third London Marathon. **SUCCESS**

9 Thank you for the flowers. That was very ______ of you. **THOUGHT**

10 You have a very ______ attitude. You should try to accept other people's opinions. **TOLERANCE**

Writing

FCE Part 2

Compositions

Read the following Writing Part 2 instructions.

Your class has been working on a project on traditional customs and celebrations. Now your teacher has asked you to write a composition giving your opinion on the following statement:

Traditional celebrations have no relevance in today's world and are a waste of time and money.

Write your **composition** in **120–180** words.

A Model

Read the example composition below, and then complete each of the spaces with one of the words in the box.

however	extent	think	although	argument
conclude	moreover	hand	opinion	

Every country has its own traditions, some of which have existed for centuries. In my **(1)** ______________ we should do everything possible to preserve them.

Some people **(2)** ______________ that in today's high-tech world traditional celebrations are too old-fashioned and irrelevant to our lives. **(3)** ______________, events such as Carnival are important, as they bring communities together and make us think about other people and not just computers.

Another **(4)** ______________ against traditional festivals is that they are expensive to organise. To some **(5)** ______________ this is true, particularly when there are firework displays or parades. On the other **(6)** ______________, it is a small price to pay for brightening up our lives with entertainment and colour. **(7)** ______________, celebrations like the 'Fallas' in my home town of Valencia attract many tourists and their money.

Finally, **(8)** ______________ I agree that some traditional customs have lost their original significance, they can provide an opportunity for us to learn about our past. For example, Bonfire Night teaches British children about a particular period of their country's history.

To **(9)** ______________, traditional celebrations are a source of great pleasure and interest, and they are certainly worth keeping.

Which words in the composition above are used to introduce the three examples of traditional celebrations?

B Organization

Which of these paragraph plans does the example composition follow?

A	B
1 Introduction: writer's general opinion	**1** Introduction: writer's general opinion
2 First point for the statement	**2** First point for the statement and writer's argument against this point.
3 Second point for the statement	**3** Second point for the statement and writer's argument against this point.
4 Third point for the statement	**4** Third point for the statement and writer's argument against this point.
5 Conclusion: writer states opinion	**5** Conclusion: writer states opinion again

C Ideas

Read these three statements which were given to a class as composition titles.

A *Sport today has become far too competitive and is no longer enjoyable.*
B *Village life is more pleasant than city life*
C *All students should spend a year working before they go to university.*

Match the following ideas to the appropriate statement and then say whether the students who wrote them agreed or disagreed with the statement. The first one has been done for you.

1 It's big business now – there's too much money involved. ***A*** *(agree)*
2 There's nothing to do there. It's so dull and boring.
3 You might do a job which is completely irrelevant to what you do after university.
4 People don't socialize like they do in the city.
5 Athletes never used to take drugs. Breaking world records doesn't mean anything now.
6 You'd be taking away jobs from unemployed people.
7 Violence at football matches is just one example of the way some people take it too seriously.
8 It sounds like a waste of time. I can't see how it would make me a better person.
9 It's not as quiet as you might think – all those animals waking you up every morning.
10 Employers would probably use it as a way of getting cheap labour.
11 Sport is controlled by politicians, who use it to make their country look better than others.
12 It gets busy and crowded at the weekend because everyone from the city goes there to get away from it all.

D Writing task

Now write a **composition** of **120–180** words giving your opinion on **one** of the three statements **A**, **B** or **C** in section 3 above.

How to go about it

1. Choose one of the statements and write down arguments for (in favour of) it and arguments against it. You may use the ideas in section 3 above.
2. Decide whether you agree or disagree with the statement, then write a paragraph plan, using plan B in section 2 above. Try to include examples to support your arguments.
3. Decide which linking words you are going to use. You will find more in the Coursebook in the Writing sections for Units 3 and 8.
4. Write your composition.

10 Nothing but the truth

Reading

FCE Part 4

Multiple matching

1 You are going to read a newspaper article about techniques used by thieves. For questions **1–12**, choose from the people **(A–D)**. The people may be chosen more than once. When more than one answer is required, these may be given in any order. There is an example at the beginning **(0)**.

A Steve Haysham
B Pauleen Woodcock
C William Walker
D Steven Nicholls

Which of the people suggest the following?

I was shortly going to be leaving the city.	**0** *D*	
I suspected something was wrong.	**1**	**2**
It was not as serious as it might have been.	**3**	
I had problems understanding them.	**4**	
It made me suspicious for the rest of my visit.	**5**	
I gave them the impression I had been taken in.	**6**	
I did not fall for the trick.	**7**	**8**
My actions made it obvious I was not a local.	**9**	
I gave a small reward.	**10**	
Something which smelled bad was used to create confusion.	**11**	
I became aware something was wrong much later.	**12**	

Travellers' Tales
Hanging on to your Money

When I reported the incident of how three men recently attempted to rob me at Krakow bus station, several readers got in touch with their own stories.

Steve Haysham reports an experience in Manhattan: 'We were sitting on a park bench and I was carrying a large camera bag over my shoulder. When a group of teenagers ran past and around us, I held tightly onto the camera thinking this might be more than just youngsters having fun.

'Five minutes later, somebody pointed to the back of my jacket and held their nose – when I took off the jacket, the back was covered in a wet, sticky substance with an unpleasant odour. At this point we got lucky – a shop assistant came out, invited us in to clean up and told us what had happened: the kids we saw had squirted my back with something like washing-up liquid that sticks and makes a mess. In the confusion, many people put their bag down to take their jacket off and the bag is snatched when they are least expecting it.'

A similar incident happened to **Pauleen Woodcock** in New Delhi: 'I was standing near the Palika bazaar when two young men walked up to me. One drew attention to a mess of some kind on my sandal. They took me to a very conveniently located shoe cleaner and told me it would be 150 rupees (£3) to clean the sandal.

'The young men were unaware that, although white, I speak Hindi as I have Indian relatives by marriage. I let the shoe cleaner do his work with the young men there, and offered him the usual payment of 50 rupees. When they tried to protest, I spoke to them in Hindi, at which point they realized they had picked the wrong person.'

2 Match each of the words on the left with its meaning on the right. The line numbers are given in brackets.

1 pointed (6)	**a** drew attention to something by holding out a finger
2 squirted (11)	**b** taken quickly
3 sticks (12)	**c** covered with a liquid (from a tube or similar)
4 snatched (14)	**d** moving the hand from side to side
5 unaware (22)	**e** becomes attached
6 waving (51)	**f** not conscious or knowing

3 In sentences **1–8** below complete each of the spaces with the appropriate form of one of the words in **2**.

1 As she walked out of the hotel, a man _________ her bag from her and ran off.
2 We used to use an old washing-up liquid bottle to _________ water at each other.
3 She was shouting excitedly, _________ her certificate in the air.
4 _________ that he was being filmed by a CCTV camera, McGuire broke into the shop.
5 She sat on some chewing gum and it _________ to her jeans.
6 He _________ at the door and told me to get out of his office.

4 In the reading text find two expressions, collocations or phrasal verbs for each of the following verbs. Don't forget to include any dependent prepositions or other words which are used. Two examples have been done for you.

get	*in touch with someone*	____________
hold	*one's nose*	____________
pick	____________	____________
take	____________	____________
make	____________	____________
have	____________	____________

5 Complete each of the spaces below with **two** words from the text.

1 Can you get _________ with Alex and ask him if he's coming on Friday?
2 Keep close to me and hold _________ your bag; there are a lot of pickpockets.
3 I dropped all my books in the street and a kind man helped me pick _________ .
4 John took _________ a Greek restaurant last night. We had a wonderful meal.
5 I made _________ of lending some money to Alan. He still hasn't paid me back.
6 'Do you know where Simon is?' 'No, I'm sorry. I have _________ .'

And **William Walker** reports an incident that occurred on a visit to Madrid: 'I made the mistake one morning of looking at a tourist map just near the entrance to the Plaza Mayor. A few minutes later a young man walked towards me and dropped some coins at my feet. As I helped him pick them up, a pickpocket took my wallet which was inside my buttoned-up back pocket. All this happened in the space of seconds and I didn't feel a thing. Not until I got back to my hotel in the evening did I realize what had happened. Luckily I had left my credit cards in the hotel so I didn't suffer too much inconvenience, but I was left feeling angry and paranoid for what remained of my stay.'

Steven Nicholls tells of an incident in Italy: 'I was in Florence and preparing to move to Venice. I had been to the station to check the train times for the next day and was walking back towards my hotel when two women approached and pushed a newspaper under my eyes. They spoke quickly and excitedly, pointing violently at a photograph in the paper; I had no idea what they were on about so I just smiled and moved on. A sixth sense made me feel for my wallet, which, of course, was gone.

'Naturally, the women had disappeared, but a man was hurrying towards me waving my wallet! He turned out to be a local who had seen what was happening and had managed to snatch the wallet back from them. All it cost me was a Campari and soda.'

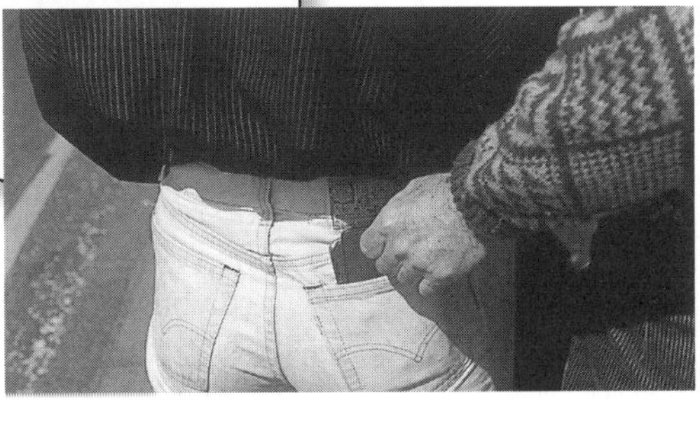

Vocabulary

Wordlist on page 204 of the Coursebook

A Crime

Match each of the following descriptions with a crime from the box.

burglary	blackmail	pickpocketing	kidnap
smuggling	arson	robbery	drug trafficking

1 By the time he realized his wallet was missing, it was too late. The bus had stopped and the two men had run off in different directions. ______________

2 Police have found evidence which suggests the building may have been burned down by an ex-employee who was sacked from the company three months ago. ______________

3 Three armed men, each wearing a stocking over his head, ordered the customers to lie still on the floor while the cashier emptied the safe. ______________

4 We must have left a window open. They took the video, the television and all my jewellery. The neighbours didn't hear a thing. ______________

5 Mrs Brandon received a note demanding £1 million in return for the release of her husband. ______________

6 To escape detection he would go to the local cyber café to email his demands. He wanted regular monthly payments of £3,000 in return for his silence over the politician's affair with his secretary. ______________

7 For two years he had been illegally taking religious icons and other art treasures out of the country in order to sell them to art collectors in Western Europe. ______________

8 Police suspected that most of his fortune came from trading in narcotics, yet they had difficulty proving it. ______________

B Phrasal verbs

Phrasal verb list on pages 122 and 123

1 Use the following verbs and particles to make phrasal verbs which have the same meanings as the definitions in **1–8**.

Verbs:	take	make	look	get		
Particles:	up	in	out	up to	into	away with

1 trick or deceive ______________
2 investigate ______________
3 not be punished for something ______________
4 see, hear or understand with difficulty ______________
5 invent (a story, an excuse) ______________
6 start doing ______________
7 admire and respect ______________
8 do things you know you shouldn't ______________

2 Complete the spaces with the appropriate forms of the phrasal verbs above.

1 Is this story true or are you ______________ it ______________ ?
2 I couldn't ______________ what he was saying. I think he was drunk.
3 He said he'd been robbed and needed some money for a taxi, but I wasn't ______________ by his story.
4 You're a fool if you think you can drive so fast all the time and ______________ it.
5 The police are ______________ the causes of the accident.
6 Are you in trouble with the police again? What have you been ______________ this time?

Language focus

Grammar reference on pages 213 and 214 of the Coursebook

A Active and passive

Complete each of the spaces with an appropriate active or passive form of the verb in brackets. You may need to use more than one word in each space.

1 Glenn Lambert ______________ (release) from prison yesterday, ten years after ______________ (find) guilty of a crime he ______________ (not commit).

2 Our car ______________ (repair) at the garage at the moment. I ______________ (tell) yesterday that it probably ______________ (not be) ready until next Friday.

3 **a:** I ______________ (ask) to give a talk at the conference next month.
b: So have I. I ______________ (not prepare) mine yet. How about you?

4 **a:** What ______________ (happen) to those boys who ______________ (catch) spraying paint on the walls of the school last year?
b: Don't you remember? They ______________ (make) to clean it all off. It ______________ (take) them three days altogether.

5 Three million chocolate bars ______________ (produce) at this factory each week. Over one million of these ______________ (sell) in the UK, and the rest ______________ (export) to other European countries.

6 My great grandfather ______________ (give) a beautiful clock when he retired in 1960. When he ______________ (die) in 1980, the clock ______________ (stop) working; it still ______________ (not fix).

7 A Roman necklace, which ______________ (think) to be worth over two million pounds, ______________ (find) last week by Audrey Perham while she ______________ (walk) her dog in Queen's Park, Brighton.

8 There were two of them, both about ten years old. They came into my garden and ______________ (destroy) all the flowers. The police ______________ (not do) anything. It's not right – they shouldn't ______________ (allow) to get away with it!

B Revision: Modal verbs

Complete each of the spaces with one of the negative modal forms from the box, together with the correct form of the verb in brackets. More than one answer may be possible.

mustn't don't have to	don't need to didn't need to	shouldn't didn't have to	needn't needn't have

1 What a waste of time! I ______________ (revise) 16th century European history; none of it came up in the exam.
2 We ______________ (pay) for a babysitter for Luke last night; my parents looked after him at their house.
3 The Christmas holidays are a little longer than usual this year. We ______________ (go) back to school until January 10th.
4 You ______________ (tell) anyone what I've just said. I'll be very angry if you do.
5 I know I ______________ (have) any more cream cakes, but it is my birthday after all.
6 I realize now, of course, that I ______________ (buy) all this wine for the party; we've got a lot of bottles left from the last one we had.
7 You ______________ (worry) about your car while you're away on holiday. We'll look after it for you.
8 He ______________ (go) to prison in the end. The judge let him off with a £900 fine.

Use of English

FCE Part 3

Transformations

Complete the second sentence so that it has a similar meaning to the first sentence, using the word given. **Do not change the word given.** You must use between two and five words, including the word given. There is an example at the beginning **(0)**.

0 My friends have invited me to their wedding.
invited
I *have been invited* to my friends' wedding.

1 No one gave me any help with the homework.
not
I ______________________ any help with the homework.

2 Someone is meeting him at the station.
met
He ______________________ at the station.

3 Thieves stole all her priceless jewels.
robbed
She ______________________ all her priceless jewels.

4 The police are investigating her disappearance.
looked
Her disappearance ______________________ by the police.

5 The witness had invented the whole story.
made
The whole story ______________________ the witness.

6 People say swimming is good exercise for your back.
said
Swimming ______________________ good exercise for your back.

7 People expect that tax cuts will be announced today.
be
Tax cuts ______________________ today.

8 People believe he won a lot of money on the lottery.
believed
He ______________________ won a lot of money on the lottery.

9 They think the burglar knew the owner of the house.
known
The burglar ______________________ the owner of the house.

10 I took my coat but it wasn't necessary as it didn't rain.
have
I ______________________ my coat as it didn't rain.

11 Fortunately, it wasn't necessary for us to go shopping last weekend.
need
Fortunately, ______________________ go shopping last weekend.

What to expect in the exam

Remember in the exam you have to write your answers on a separate sheet. You should only write the missing words, not the whole sentence.

FCE Part 5

Word formation

Use the word given in capitals at the end of each line to form a word that fits in the space in the same line. There is an example at the beginning **(0)**.

CCTV cameras

Close circuit television cameras are **(0)** _increasingly_ becoming	**INCREASE**
a fact of life in modern Britain. They can be seen in office	
(1) ________________ , shopping centres, banks,	**BUILD**
(2) ________________ areas and even parks, and it is estimated	**RESIDENT**
that the average Briton is filmed an **(3)** ________________ 200 times	**AMAZE**
a day. It is believed that CCTV leads to a **(4)** ________________ in	**REDUCE**
certain types of crime, such as car theft, **(5)** ________________ and	**ROB**
street violence. Its supporters defend it as an **(6)** ________________	**EFFECT**
way of improving security in town centres, and of helping to	
bring **(7)** ________________ to justice. Civil liberties groups, who	**CRIME**
object to the **(8)** ________________ of CCTV cameras, feel that they	**PRESENT**
constitute a serious **(9)** ________________ of privacy and say that	**INVADE**
there is little **(10)** ________________ that they reduce offending.	**EVIDENT**

FCE Part 2

Open cloze

Read the text below and think of a word which best fits each space. Use only **one** word in each space. There is an example at the beginning **(0)**.

House-sitters

Nowadays **(0)** _there_ are far too many stories of homeowners **(1)** ______________ have been away on holiday and come home to find that their house **(2)** ______________ been broken into. Unfortunately, simply locking the doors and cancelling the newspapers is **(3)** ______________ enough to keep out burglars.

A much better way to prevent your home from **(4)** ______________ burgled is to employ a professional house-sitter, either through an agency **(5)** ______________ as 'Homesitters', **(6)** ______________ by placing an advertisement in a magazine like *The Lady*. House-sitters **(7)** ______________ paid around £10 **(8)** ______________ day, including a food allowance, to live in a house while **(9)** ______________ owners are away. An extra charge **(10)** ______________ made if the house-sitter is required to **(11)** ______________ care of one or more pets.

Agencies, which charge a considerable fee for their services, accept full responsibility **(12)** ______________ anything which might go wrong. House-sitters **(13)** ______________ therefore chosen very carefully; as **(14)** ______________ as the usual interview and personal references, inquiries are **(15)** ______________ about any previous criminal convictions.

Writing

FCE Part 2

Informal letters

Read the following Writing Part 2 instructions and the two answers which were written by students. Which letter do you think would be given a higher mark?

You have just returned from a holiday abroad, during which something of yours was stolen. Write a letter to your penfriend, telling him/her about the incident and what you did to try to recover the stolen item.

Student A

Dear Paul

I arrive to the station to caught the train to the airport. I feeling sad because of I finish my holiday. I enjoyed with the holiday very much and I didn't want to come to home.

I have decided to go to the shop for to buy some sweets and make me felt happier. I put my suitcase to the ground and paid to the woman for the sweets. I wanted to pick up my suitcase but it was not there any more! Where was my suitcase? What a shock! Somebody stealed it.

Consequently, I feeling sadder. It was a horrible way to finish of a holiday.

Helmut Braun

Student B

Dear Esther

How are you? Did you get my postcard from Italy? You'll never guess what happened to me after I'd posted it to you!

I was walking down the main street on my way to the beach when I heard everyone shouting behind me. I looked round and there on the pavement coming towards me was a young man on a motor scooter. Before I knew what was happening, he had snatched my bag and was riding off into the distance.

I started to run after him but it was useless – you know how unfit I am! Anyway, at that moment a car pulled over beside me and the driver, who had seen the incident, told me to get in. We chased after the thief, and as soon as he realized he was being followed, he dropped the bag and disappeared.

You can imagine how relieved I felt. And I was so grateful to the driver – thanks to him my holiday wasn't ruined.

How about you, Esther? Did anything exciting happen on your holiday? Write and tell me all about it.

Lots of love

Angela

A Analysis

Now read the two letters again and then answer Yes or No to the following questions about each one.

	A	B
Content		
1 Has the writer answered all parts of the question?		
Organization and cohesion		
2 Is the letter organized into suitable paragraphs?		
3 Are ideas connected with appropriate linking words?		
4 Does the letter have an appropriate beginning and ending?		
Range and accuracy		
5 Is there a good range of vocabulary?		
6 Has the writer used a variety of tenses?		
7 Is the English reasonably accurate?		
Style and format		
8 Is the letter written in an informal style?		
9 Is the answer clearly set out as a letter?		
Target reader		
10 Would the reader understand what happened and know what the writer did to try to recover the stolen item?		

B Accuracy

Look back at Student A's answer. Find the following mistakes and correct them:

a eight mistakes related to verb forms, eg *I arrived*

b eight mistakes related to the incorrect use of prepositions, eg ***at** the station*

C Addressing the reader

Look back at Student B's answer. Underline those sentences in which the writer talks directly to the reader of the letter.

Example:
How are you?

D Writing task

Now write your own answer to the question.

Don't forget!

- Set your answer out as an informal letter.
  Include suitable opening and closing paragraphs.
  See page 10 in Unit 1 of the Coursebook for useful language.
- Use a range of vocabulary and structures when describing what happened.
  See pages 50 and 51 in Unit 4 of the Coursebook for the ingredients of a good narrative.
- Organize your ideas into logical paragraphs. You could have one paragraph to describe how the item was stolen and another to say how you tried to recover it.

11 What on Earth's going on?

Reading

FCE Part 3

Gapped text

1 You are going to read a newspaper article about a man who teaches survival techniques. Eight sentences have been removed from the article. Choose from the sentences **A–I** the one which fits each space **(1–7)**. There is one extra sentence which you do not need to use. There is an example at the beginning **(0)**.

The man who can survive anywhere

Ray Mears tells Graham Hadley how learning survival skills can help us rediscover nature.

Armed with little more than a hunting knife and a cooking pot Ray Mears can survive anywhere. He loves nothing more than spending days, weeks or even months alone in the wild, and he will talk passionately about any aspect of the natural world, from his favourite trees to endangered species of animals. **0** I Those who sign up for the courses range from children to grandparents, with a large number of twenty to thirty-year-olds looking for a taste of adventure.

'People might see it as survival skills,' he says, 'but I aim to teach a little more than that. **1** ____ Some who have participated on the course have experienced a very profound change in their life. They develop a greater awareness of nature. They return to the cities and notice the seasons change for the first time. **2** ____ The city and their life in it are transformed.'

The Woodlore courses take participants to experience tribal life with the native people of Namibia, or to shiver through an Arctic survival course in Lapland. **3** ____ These are the places to fulfil the schoolboy dream of lighting fires with just a couple of sticks.

4 ____ 'There are lots of simple survival tips, like it's often better to avoid anything which is green. More energy is used up eating it than you get out of it. Roots are best because you need carbohydrates.'

There is a very serious purpose to what Mears does. 'All around the world cultures are losing ancient skills as the latest generation is attracted away from the land to an easy life through technology,' he explains. 'We live in a world where we can have whatever we want, but along the way we have lost contact with the natural world. **5** ____ Without them, there's a danger we could lose sight of where we've come from.'

'The area around London is particularly threatened. **6** ____ People need places where they can get close to nature.'

But Mears is not against the latest technological developments and is well aware of the benefits. **7** ____ 'In this way people can become part of a global tribe, one which lives both for and from the natural world.'

www.raymears.com

A Mears even takes groups to visit a highly-protected nature reserve in Canada to watch bear cubs being born and raised.

B He has just hired an Internet consultancy firm to design a website which will give people all over the globe access to his knowledge.

C I try to show people how to reconnect with nature, how to see it in a different light.

D This experience, and others like it, led Mears to write *The Survival Handbook*, which was published in 1989.

E The ancient woodlands should be left alone, and areas not needed for agriculture should be planted with trees and allowed to grow wild.

F They see the geese, the pigeons, the edible plants growing between the cracks in the pavement.

G These ancient skills help to put us back in touch with nature, and to understand our place in the world.

H He also teaches how to identify edible plants for food.

I His passions are reflected in Woodlore, a series of courses in which he passes on survival techniques to people of all ages.

2 Use the word given in capitals at the end of each line to form a word that fits in the space in the same line. All the words you require appeared in the reading text. There is an example at the beginning **(0)**.

0 Global warming is thought to be responsible for some of the world's recent *natural* disasters. **NATURE**

1 We took part in a demonstration yesterday to protest against the construction of two new housing ______________ on the edge of town. **DEVELOP**

2 The creation of nature reserves will help to ensure the ______________ of many endangered species. **SURVIVE**

3 There were over 350 ______________ on the Environmental Skills course. **PARTICIPATE**

4 He spoke ______________ about the need to protect the tiger's natural habitat. **PASSION**

5 Deforestation in South America is an issue of ______________ importance. **GLOBE**

6 You can't really go ______________ in the countryside nowadays without seeing some evidence of Man's influence. **WHERE**

7 The council intends to raise ______________ of the effects of traffic pollution on our health. **AWARE**

8 Recent ______________ advances such as the Internet are proving very useful for conservationists. **TECHNOLOGY**

3 In numbers **1–3** in excercise **2** you needed to use the suffixes *-ment, -al* and *-ant* to form the appropriate nouns. Use these same suffixes to form nouns from the following verbs. The first two have been done for you.

Verb	Noun	Verb	Noun
arrive	*arrival*	enjoy	____________
consult	*consultant*	replace	____________
entertain	____________	approve	____________
refuse	____________	deny	____________
assist	____________	arrange	____________
occupy	____________	inhabit	____________

4 Complete each of the spaces with the correct form of one of the nouns in exercise **3**.

1 All 540 ____________ of the village of Poynings had to be evacuated because of the forest fire.
2 The Government has given its ____________ for the construction of a new by-pass for Oldbury. Road works will start next April.
3 The views were fantastic but the constant noise of the motorway did rather ruin our ____________ of the walk.
4 Conservationists were not convinced by the Minister's ____________ that radioactive waste had been dumped at sea.
5 Fortunately, none of the ____________ of the car was injured in the crash.

Vocabulary

Wordlist on pages 204 and 205 of the Coursebook

A Crossword: The weather

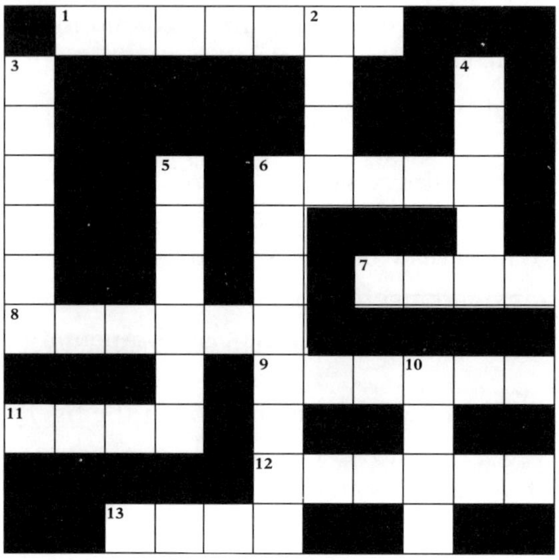

Across

1 a long period of time without rain
6 a large amount of water covering an area which is normally dry
7 a very strong wind
8 a ________ storm is a very bad one
9 a ________ sea has lots of small waves caused by the wind
11 ________ rain consists of very small raindrops
12 'Several trees were ________ by lightning during the storm.'
13 a ________ is a short, sudden period of strong wind

Down

2 small hard balls of frozen rain
3 'Look at those thick, black ________ – I think it's going to rain.'
4 'After the earthquake came a ________ wave, which destroyed several houses on the coast.'
5 a gentle ________ is a very light wind
6 'You can't always rely on the weather ________ to predict the weather accurately.'
10 'to ________ with rain' means 'to rain very heavily'

B The environment

1 Match each sentence beginning **1–6** with an appropriate ending **a–f**.

1 One of the aims of Greenpeace is to **raise**
2 I strongly believe that anyone caught **dropping**
3 The ship's captain denied he had been **dumping**
4 Several species of birds and animals **face**
5 The local authorities talk of the need to **recycle**
6 Not enough is being done to **preserve**

a **extinction** in this country as a result of modern farming methods.
b **paper**, but they have not provided enough containers to enable us to do this.
c **awareness** of the environmental problems facing our planet.
d **litter** should be ordered to pay a heavy fine.
e **wildlife** in this country.
f **waste** of any kind at sea.

2 Match the words **1–8** with the words **a–h** to form compound nouns.

1 bottle	**a** effect
2 dog	**b** pollution
3 greenhouse	**c** reserve
4 oil	**d** mess
5 traffic	**e** bank
6 exhaust	**f** slick
7 power	**g** station
8 nature	**h** fumes

3 Complete each of the spaces with one of the compound nouns from exercise **2**.

1 ________________ are responsible for a great deal of the pollution in our cities.
2 The huge ________________ is moving slowly towards Ireland, and several miles of coastline are under threat.
3 It's almost impossible to walk on the pavement in this city without stepping in ________________ .
4 Global warming is caused by the ________________ , the result of an increase in the amount of carbon dioxide and other gases in the Earth's atmosphere.
5 Environmentalists have been protesting at the construction of a new nuclear ________________ on the outskirts of the city.
6 Wildlife enthusiasts have called for the area to be made a ________________ in order to protect the rare species of butterfly which lives there.

Language focus

Grammar reference on pages 214 and 215 of the Coursebook

A *So*, *neither* and *nor*

1 Match each statement **1–8** with a reply **a–h**.

1 She doesn't like that type of music.	**a** So would I.
2 We didn't enjoy the film.	**b** I'm not.
3 I went swimming last night.	**c** Neither does he.
4 My favourite food is pasta.	**d** So did my brother.
5 She's never been abroad.	**e** Neither did they.
6 I'd rather go to the cinema.	**f** We don't.
7 He's going to the demonstration.	**g** Neither have I.
8 I have to do a lot of homework tonight.	**h** So is mine.

2 Complete each of the spaces below with *so* or *neither/nor* and an appropriate auxiliary verb. The first one has been done for you.

1 He can't drive and neither can I.
2 I'm older than Harry, and ______________ Ron.
3 He never writes to me, and ______________ Colin.
4 Her parents are going to France, and ______________ mine.
5 Seamus came to the party, and ______________ Dean.
6 Hermione won't tell anyone, and ______________ I.
7 I've already seen that film, and ______________ Neville.
8 I wouldn't be happy if you went alone, and ______________ your father.
9 I'd better go to bed, and ______________ you, young man.

B Conditionals

1 Complete the spaces in the following sentences with the appropriate form of the verb in brackets. The first one has been done for you.

1 If I *had* (have) more time, I *would help* (help) you, but I'm afraid I'm just too busy.
2 I ________________ (buy) you a new pair of football boots as long as you ________________ (promise) to look after them properly.
3 Why did you tell your parents? If you ________________ (not/say) anything, we ________________ (not/get) into trouble.
4 If he ________________ (sleep) for less than eight hours, he ________________ (usually/be) bad-tempered all morning.
5 It's a shame you weren't at the party. If you ________________ (go), you ________________ (meet) my sister.
6 If we ________________ (beat) United next Saturday, we ________________ (go) to the top of the league.
7 There's a quicker way to do it. If you ________________ (press) 'control' and 'U', it ________________ (underline) your work as you type.
8 If I ________________ (be) you, I ________________ (go) to the doctor's.
9 We ________________ (be) there by 6 o'clock this evening unless we ________________ (get) stuck in a traffic jam.
10 I had to wait two hours to see the doctor. If I ________________ (not/take) my book with me to read, I ________________ (get) so bored.

2 Rewrite sentences below to form second, third or mixed conditional sentences. The first one has been done for you.

1 I don't have to pay to get into the museum because I'm unemployed.

If I wasn't unemployed, I'd have to pay to get into the museum.

2 We didn't go sailing because there wasn't enough wind.

____

3 We don't go abroad on holiday because I'm afraid of flying.

____

4 He's broken his leg so he can't drive.

____

5 I couldn't take any photos because I forgot to pack my camera.

____

6 He isn't going to the wedding because he hasn't got a suit.

____

7 He's feeling ill because he drank too much last night.

____

8 She didn't pass her exams so she couldn't go to university.

____

9 They didn't watch the news so they didn't hear about the earthquake.

____

3 Complete each of the following sentences in an appropriate way.

1 If I had to spend a year living abroad, I ______________________ .
2 If I had the power to change one thing in my country, I ______________________ .
3 I probably wouldn't have met my best friend if ______________________ .
4 I'd be really pleased if ______________________ .
5 If someone gives me some money for my birthday, ______________________ .
6 If the computer hadn't been invented, ______________________ .

Use of English

FCE Part 1

Multiple choice cloze

Read the text below and decide which answer **A**, **B**, **C** or **D** best fits each space. There is an example at the beginning **(0)**.

Global warming

Few people now **(0)** _*question*_ the reality of global warming and its effects on the world's climate. Many scientists **(1)** ________ the blame for recent natural disasters on the increase **(2)** ________ the world's temperatures and are convinced that, more than **(3)** ________ before, the Earth is at **(4)** ________ from the forces of the wind, rain and sun. **(5)** ________ to them, global warming is making extreme weather events, **(6)** ________ as hurricanes and droughts, even more **(7)** ________ and causing sea levels all around the world to **(8)** ________ .
Environmental groups are putting **(9)** ________ on governments to take action to reduce the **(10)** ________ of carbon dioxide which is given **(11)** ________ by factories and power plants, thus attacking the problem at its source. They are in **(12)** ________ of more money being spent on research into solar, wind and wave energy devices, which could then replace existing power **(13)** ________ .
Some scientists, **(14)** ________ , believe that even if we stopped releasing carbon dioxide and other gases into the atmosphere tomorrow, we would have to wait **(15)** ________ hundred years to notice the results. Global warming, it seems, is here to stay.

0	**A** hesitate	**B** _question_	**C** disagree	**D** concern
1	**A** give	**B** put	**C** take	**D** have
2	**A** in	**B** at	**C** by	**D** to
3	**A** yet	**B** never	**C** once	**D** ever
4	**A** threat	**B** danger	**C** risk	**D** harm
5	**A** Concerning	**B** Regarding	**C** Depending	**D** According
6	**A** such	**B** just	**C** even	**D** well
7	**A** strict	**B** severe	**C** strong	**D** heavy
8	**A** raise	**B** arise	**C** rise	**D** lift
9	**A** force	**B** pressure	**C** persuasion	**D** encouragement
10	**A** amount	**B** deal	**C** number	**D** count
11	**A** off	**B** away	**C** up	**D** over
12	**A** belief	**B** request	**C** favour	**D** suggestion
13	**A** factories	**B** generations	**C** houses	**D** stations
14	**A** but	**B** although	**C** despite	**D** however
15	**A** several	**B** over	**C** numerous	**D** various

FCE Part 4

Error correction

Read the text below and look carefully at each line. Some of the lines are correct, and some have a word which should not be there. If a line is correct, put a tick (✓) at the end of the line. If a line has a word which should not be there, write the word. There are two examples at the beginning (**0** and **00**).

Bad weather

0	I'm writing to you from our hotel room on the Mediterranean island of	✓
00	Mallorca. Unfortunately, I can't to tell you very much about the island	*to*
1	because we've had such a terrible weather that we've hardly been out of	______
2	the hotel since we have arrived. On our very first day here the sky was	______
3	overcast and the temperature was about twenty degrees, much lower than	______
4	normal is at this time of the year. Then, the next day, we woke up to the	______
5	sound like of torrential rain beating against the windows, and it's been	______
6	pouring with almost non stop ever since. We'd have brought more books	______
7	and games with us if we would had known it was going to be like this –	______
8	the kids are beginning to get bored with playing cards all the time. Poor	______
9	Katie was really looking forward to go swimming in the sea, but it's far	______
10	too rough for that and she can't even go in the pool, which it has been	______
11	closed. The weather forecast says us that it should begin to improve by	______
12	the end of the week, but some of the shopkeepers we've spoken to in the	______
13	town of Palma aren't so much optimistic – they think it might well go on	______
14	raining for longer. We've decided that unless it will brightens up in the	______
15	next few days, we'll probably come home a week earlier than had planned.	______

Writing

FCE Part 2

Articles

1 Read the following Writing Part 2 question and the model below.

You see this announcement in an international magazine:

WRITING COMPETITION

The Best and the Worst
The theme of our writing competition this month is **The Weather**.
Write an article about your favourite and least favourite weather conditions, telling our readers why you feel the way you do.
The best article will be published in the magazine and the writer will receive £250

Write your **article** for the magazine.

The highs and lows of mountain weather

If you lived in the mountains like me, what would be your favourite type of weather? Glorious sunshine to sunbathe in? Deep snow to ski in?

Surprisingly, perhaps, it's the rain I most enjoy. Whether it's fine or heavy, spitting or pouring, I love wet weather! The rain on my face as I walk across the fields is cool and refreshing and always puts me in a good mood. It makes me feel optimistic about the future: after the rain, the sun comes out; after a shower the countryside is greener; and after my walk there's the promise of a warm fire and a cup of hot cocoa.

And what would you find it hard to put up with? Where I live it's the wind, which blows almost continuously for two weeks every August. Clothes are blown off washing lines, tiles are pulled off roofs and activities such as walking and cycling become very difficult. Who wouldn't feel bad-tempered by the end of it all?

But whatever the weather, I know I'd hate it if it was always the same.

2 The model is written in a more informal style. Find examples in the article of the following features.

Features	Examples
• A relevant title	*The highs and lows of mountain weather*
• Questions to involve the reader	______________
• A range of vocabulary related to the weather	______________
• Elements of informal language eg *contractions, phrasal verbs, linking words*	______________
• Examples to illustrate a point	______________
• Adverbs expressing opinion or attitude	______________

3 Either: **a** Write your own answer to the question in 1 on page 88
or **b** Write an answer to **one** of the following questions.

1 You see this announcement in an international magazine:

> **COMPETITION**
>
> **Write an article about a situation when you experienced severe weather conditions, telling our readers how you were affected by them.**
>
> **The best article will win a prize of £500.**

Write your **article** for the competition.

2 You see this notice in an international magazine:

> **PEOPLE AND PLACES**
>
> We are looking for articles on the following question:
>
> *How does the climate in your country affect the way people feel and behave?*
>
> The best article will be published in our magazine.

Write your **article** for the magazine.

Before you write

- Read more about writing articles on pages 215 and 216 of the Coursebook.
- Read the following advice about style and do the exercise below.

Formal and Informal Style: consistency

In each of the questions above, the article will be written for readers of an international magazine. The style of your writing can be either more formal or more informal, but it must be consistent throughout the article; in other words, you should not mix formal and informal language in the same piece of writing.

4 The following extracts **a–c** were each written in answer to one of the three writing questions above. Match each extract to one of the questions. Which of the extracts is **not** written in a consistent style?

a

I've never really been keen on going out in the snow - and I can't understand why people get so excited about it. Your feet get soaking wet, your fingers nearly freeze off, and where's the fun in having a snowball pushed down the back of your neck? I'd love to have enough money to be able to get away from here when it snows.

b

Moreover, the combination of harsh winters and warm summers has an interesting effect on the personality of those who live in the more remote, rural parts of my country. Inhabitants of these areas tend to withdraw into themselves between December and March, becoming shy and reserved. In spring, however, they undergo a transformation - it's really amazing! They're just so incredibly different - you'd almost think you were in another country!

c

Huge waves crashed onto the beach, sending sand and stones high into the air. Gale-force winds caused destruction to buildings along the seafront and made walking in the street extremely hazardous. We spent the day sheltering in the lounge area of our hotel, wondering when, if ever, the storm would die down.

12 Looking after yourself

Reading

FCE Part 2

Multiple choice

1 You are going to read a magazine article about a chef. For questions **1–7**, choose the answer **A**, **B**, **C** or **D** which you think fits best according to the text.

Meals on *wheels*

Sheila Keating meets the Ferrari team chef at a Formula One race.

It's Grand Prix weekend, and as the stars of Formula One race against the clock to give themselves the best starting position for the big event tomorrow, a different race against time is under way. In miniature makeshift kitchens alongside the track, the team chefs are busy preparing lunch for the mechanics and drivers.

Claudio Degli Esposti is in charge of the cooking for all 60 Ferrari team members, plus their personal weekend guests, who could bring the numbers up to 80. 'It's a huge honour to be chef of the Ferrari team,' he says. 'I get on really well with the guys, and they make me feel part of things. Also you have the chance to travel all over the world. I don't see a great deal of the racing,' he says, laughing, 'but the TV monitor is on just outside the kitchen, so I know what's going on.'

The food he prepares for the team is typical of his region in Italy, Emilia Romagna, where the team is based: lasagne, tortelloni, tortellini, ravioli. 'There are usually two different pastas, two or three kinds of meat, plenty of side dishes,' he explains. It is left to others to say that the food at Ferrari is the envy of other teams. Degli Esposti simply shrugs his shoulders and smiles. 'Italians enjoy eating good food. It is a way of life, so even if your focus is on winning the world championship, you must still have good food.'

The drivers, of course, have their own long-term food agenda, tailored to the stresses of competition. With temperatures in the cockpit of a Formula One car sometimes 15 degrees hotter than that outside, it is not unusual for a driver to lose three kilos in fluid during a race, unless he has the right balance of fluid and carbohydrate. Driver Michael Schumacher, with his reputation for formidable fitness, is attended at all times by Balbir Singh, who looks after his diet and exercise. 'Before qualifying and racing, Michael eats the food prepared by Singh,' says Degli Esposti, 'usually something very light, but afterwards he eats the same food as the rest of the team.'

Unlike many of the team kitchens, which contain stacks of tins and jars, Degli Esposti's has a large fridge filled with different types of cheese, ham, sausages, vegetables and fruit. The emphasis is on simple food prepared carefully. 'In the beginning it was very difficult, working in a very small kitchen, without a lot of the things a chef is used to. And finding ingredients was a problem. Now I know the places to shop at near every track, and I know I can get anything I need. I love to cook fish and meat, but unless I can get the best, I don't touch it.'

Lunch is spread out as a buffet. On a table at one end of the eating area there are salads of mozzarella and tomatoes, carpaccio topped with truffles, Italian sausages and courgettes, a chicken dish with rosemary potatoes, and tortellini tossed in a sauce of cheese and cream. 'I always try to get as much as possible prepared early, so I have only the hot dishes to do at the last minute,' explains Degli Esposti. The mechanics come in first, followed closely by the drivers. Eddie Irvine heads straight for the truffles, while Schumacher wanders into the kitchen to see what's cooking.

Lunch over, everyone disperses, full of praise for the chef. Degli Esposti gives a small wave of appreciation and immediately starts clearing away. 'I have many friends in Italy,' he says quietly, 'who think I have the best job in the world.'

1 What does Degli Esposti enjoy about his job?
A He can see motor racing all over the world.
B He likes being a member of a team.
C He can travel around the countries he visits.
D He is a fan of Formula One racing.

2 What does the writer mean when she says that the drivers 'have their own long-term food agenda' in lines 40 and 41?
A They spend a lot of time eating.
B They eat the same things all season.
C They go for long periods without eating.
D They follow a carefully planned diet.

3 Schumacher eats food prepared by Balbir Singh because
A he prefers it to Degli Esposti's.
B it forms an important part of his preparation for a race.
C it has an excellent reputation.
D it contains more fluids and carbohydrates than Degli Esposti's.

4 The food in Degli Esposti's kitchen, compared to that in other teams' kitchens, is
A fresher.
B easier to cook.
C more varied.
D less fattening.

5 What does Degli Esposti insist on when he is cooking for the Ferrari team?
A nearby shops
B a big kitchen
C the highest quality food
D a large fridge

6 When the members of the Ferrari team have lunch
A they go into the kitchen to get their food.
B they all eat at the same table.
C they serve themselves.
D they each eat a number of different dishes.

7 Which adjective would the writer use to describe Degli Esposti?
A modest
B shy
C arrogant
D moody

2 Complete the spaces with an appropriate preposition. The words in **bold** appear in the text.

1 It was a **race** __________ **the clock** to get the menus printed in time for the opening.
2 In a restaurant the maitre d' is the person __________ **charge** __________ all the waiters.
3 It's **typical** __________ you to order the most expensive dish in the restaurant!
4 Welcome to *Food Matters*. In tonight's programme the **focus** is __________ Mediterranean food.
5 John has a **reputation** __________ eating too quickly.
6 Ravioli is usually **filled** __________ minced meat or cheese.
7 The **emphasis** in this restaurant is __________ quality, not quantity.
8 All the wedding guests were full of **praise** __________ the chef.

Vocabulary

Wordlist on page 205 of the Coursebook

A Food

Which word could be used to describe the food in each of the following cases? Match each of the words in the box to a statement. The first one has been done for you.

spicy	rich	~~bitter~~	sour	stodgy	sickly	crunchy	bland	savoury	greasy

1 This coffee really needs a little more sugar adding to it. ___*bitter*___
2 There's rather a lot of fat on these chips. __________
3 How many litres of cream did you put in this sauce? __________
4 No, it's not a sweet dish. It's got salt and a few herbs in it. __________
5 I'm sorry, I don't like this – it's like eating a lemon. __________
6 That chocolate mousse was far too sweet – it made me feel quite ill. __________
7 Sorry about thc noise – this celery's just so fresh. __________
8 I'm not very keen on curry; it's too hot for me. __________
9 The food in our school canteen is very heavy; it takes ages to digest. __________
10 It hasn't really got a lot of flavour, has it? __________

B Health

Read the definitions below, then complete each space **1–6** with an appropriate form of one of the words.

wound (n)
a cut or hole in the body, often caused by a gun, knife or other weapon. (verb: wound)

injury (n)
harm caused to a person, often as the result of an accident (verb: injure)

damage (n)
harm caused to things (verb: damage)

ache (n)
a dull continuous pain (verb: ache)

pain (n)
usually more extreme discomfort than ache, caused by injury or illness

hurt (v)
to cause pain to (part of) a person

1 A total of sixteen houses were ______________ in the explosion.
2 Let go of my arm – you're ______________ me!
3 Take an aspirin if your head ______________ .
4 The robbers shot at security guards, killing one and seriously ______________ another.
5 Several people received serious ______________ in the train crash.
6 He complained of chest ______________ and breathing difficulties – a sure sign of pneumonia.

C *Have*, *put*, *give* and *take*

Match each sentence beginning on the left with a suitable ending on the right.

1 He had both	**a** plaster on her cut.
2 He had another	**b** an injection in his leg.
3 They put him	**c** own temperature.
4 She put a	**d** operation on his leg.
5 They gave him	**e** his legs in plaster for six weeks.
6 He gave her	**f** pill for her headache.
7 She took a	**g** on a course of antibiotics.
8 He took his	**h** a prescription, which she took to the chemist's.

D Word formation: Nouns

In one word in each of the groups of four below, the wrong suffix has been used to form the noun. Find the word and write the correct form.

Example:

0 *ignorance*	*significance*	frequency ~~*frequance*~~	*resistance*

1 tiredness	involveness	friendliness	uselessness
2 inconvenience	impatience	disappearence	disobedience
3 announcement	replacement	measurement	obligement
4 seriosity	generosity	curiosity	anxiety
5 explanation	complication	comparation	investigation
6 soreness	popularness	consciousness	healthiness
7 commitment	permitment	excitement	investment
8 security	severity	sincerity	retirity

Language focus

Grammar reference on pages 215 and 216 of the Coursebook

A Countable and uncountable nouns

Underline the alternative which cannot be used.

1 Have you heard *any/a/the* news about the accident?
2 I didn't speak *a large number/a great deal/a lot* of English when I was in London.
3 *Many/Several/Every* people in our neighbourhood have complained about the smell from the factory.
4 They didn't give us very much *advice/suggestion/information* about where to look for a cheap *guest house/hotel/accommodation* in the town.
5 Could you pass me a *piece/bar/slice* of bread please?
6 **a:** Would you like *some/any/few* more chips?
b: No, thanks. I've already got *plenty/much/enough*.
7 We haven't got *no/any/much* cheese left. Could you buy *a few/a little/some* on your way home tonight?
8 Come on, let's go out for a meal. We've still got *a little/little/plenty of* money.
9 I think I'll have *some more/another/any more* coffee.
10 Don't put *too much/another/any more* chicken in my sandwiches. A couple of slices is plenty.

B Reported speech

1 Read this extract from a letter which Roger wrote to his penfriend, telling him about an interview for a job he went to recently. Then complete the dialogue below.

It was a really short interview, but I think I did OK. She started off by asking why I had applied for the job. I explained to her that I was thinking of going to catering college next year and that I wanted to have some experience of hotel or restaurant work first. Then when she asked me if I had any previous experience I told her about a summer holiday I'd spent working behind the bar at the Sussex Hotel. I mentioned something about how useful it had been and how it had helped me to understand what working in a large hotel was like. She seemed quite impressed with that! Anyway, she wanted to know what I thought my main strengths were, so I said I had a lot of patience and that I was very reliable – you know how I always work hard and never arrive late.

Interviewer: So, tell me Roger, **(1)** ______________________ ?

Roger: Well, **(2)** ______________________ to catering college next year, and **(3)** ______________________ some experience of working in a restaurant or hotel before I go.

Interviewer: And **(4)** ______________________ any previous experience of this type of work?

Roger: Yes, I spent one summer working behind the bar in the restaurant at the Sussex Hotel. It **(5)** ______________________ . I think it **(6)** ______________________ to work in a large hotel – the demands of the job, the pressures, the challenges and so on.

Interviewer: Good. Now, let's talk about your personal qualities. **(7)** ______________________ ?

Roger: Well, I **(8)** ______________________ , which I think is an important quality for a waiter. And I also think **(9)** ______________________ person – I always work hard, and I never arrive late for anything.

2 The following comments from two teachers were recorded by Lynda Johnson when doing a survey at school on healthy living. Read the questions and comments and then complete the extract from the report which Lynda wrote a week later.

What do you do to keep fit?

Mr Bracewell: I enjoy all kinds of sport, particularly running – I'm competing in a marathon tomorrow.

Ms Hallam: I do aerobics every morning, but I'm thinking of taking up jogging instead.

Can you give us any advice about what to eat?

Mr Bracewell: Personally, I eat a lot of carbohydrates because of my running, but in general, a balanced diet is the best way to stay healthy.

Ms Hallam: The advice I always give to my students is that they shouldn't eat snacks between meals. And of course, everyone should eat a balanced diet.

Do you think diets are a good way to lose weight?

Mr Bracewell: I don't know – I've never needed to go on one!

Ms Hallam: I went on a diet once and I lost about five kilos. I wouldn't do it again, though – I like eating too much.

Healthy living

As part of a project on healthy living I spoke last week to Mr Bracewell, the French teacher, and Ms Hallam, who teaches biology, and I asked them to comment on various aspects related to this topic.

Firstly, I asked both teachers what **(1)** ________________ .
Mr Bracewell said he enjoyed all kinds of sports, particularly running: he added that **(2)** ________________ . Ms Hallam said **(3)** ________________ every morning, but that **(4)** ________________ instead.

When I asked them **(5)** ________________ any advice about what to eat, both teachers recommended **(6)** ________________ a balanced diet. Ms Hallam said that she always advised **(7)** ________________ snacks between meals, and Mr Bracewell commented that he ate a lot of carbohydrates because of his running.

I then asked the teachers **(8)** ________________ a good way to lose weight. Mr Bracewell replied that he did not know, because **(9)** ________________ ________________ . Ms Hallam said that **(10)** ________________ and had lost five kilos. She went on to say that **(11)** ________________ , however, as she **(12)** ________________ too much.

Use of English

FCE Part 2

Open cloze

Read the text below and think of the word which best fits each space. Use only **one** word in each space. There is an example at the beginning **(0)**.

Perfect fish and chips

There **(0)** _are_ plenty of fish and chip shops in Hampshire, but **(1)** _______ , if any, are as popular as the one in Eastleigh, not far from Southampton. **(2)** _______ the time it opens at 5 o'clock until closing time at 9, there is an almost constant queue.

According **(3)** _______ the owners, Les and Shirley Armstrong, there are four areas that must be perfect in **(4)** _______ to achieve great fish and chips. First, of **(5)** _______ , you need the fish. The Armstrongs **(6)** _______ not use fresh cod, which Les says goes soft and mushy. Instead, **(7)** _______ buy frozen Icelandic cod, **(8)** _______ is filleted and frozen within three hours of **(9)** _______ caught. When you fry it, **(10)** _______ stays firm and comes apart in lovely white flakes. Next on the list are the potatoes. If you want to make perfect chips, Les suggests you **(11)** _______ buy potatoes with a low sugar content; too **(12)** _______ sugar and you end up with greasy, brown chips.

Then there is the batter, a mixture of flour, eggs and milk which is used **(13)** _______ cover the fish before frying it. The Armstrongs dip their fish in a combination of two types of batter; **(14)** _______ contains hard flour, the other soft. Finally, you need a good beef fat, or 'dripping'; Les and Shirley fry their fish and chips separately in a high-quality deodorized dripping that cannot **(15)** _______ smelt in the shop.

FCE Part 3

Transformations

Complete the second sentence so that it has a similar meaning to the first sentence, using the word given. **Do not change the word given**. You must use between two and five words, including the word given.

1 'You must wear a tie,' the teacher told him.
to
The teacher told him he ________________________ a tie.

2 'We were trying to phone you,' they said.
been
They said ________________________ to phone me.

3 'Where did you buy your shoes, Sally?' asked Gail.
had
Gail asked Sally ________________________ shoes.

4 'Don't swim too far out,' she warned him.
warned
She ________________________ swim too far out.

5 Sean said I ought to lie down for a while.
lie
Sean suggested ________________________ for a while.

6 She gave me very little help with the homework.
not
She did ________________________ help with my homework.

Writing

FCE Part 2

Compositions, short stories and informal letters

A Planning

Match the writing questions **1–3** to the paragraph plans **A–C**.

1 You have been doing a class project on food. Your teacher has asked you to write a composition giving your opinions on the following statement:

Parents should let their children eat what they want

Write your **composition**.

2 You have decided to enter a short story competition. The competition rules say that the story must end with the following words:

I will never forget that meal as long as I live.

Write your **story** for the competition.

3 Last weekend several of your relatives came to your home for a family meal to celebrate an important event. Write a letter to your pen friend, telling him/her what you were celebrating and describing the meal. Describe what you ate **and** mention some things that happened during the celebrations. Do not write any addresses.

Write your **letter**.

A

- 'Anniversary meal' – going out together for one year
- I arrived late – she was angry
- Food took long time to arrive; cold and undercooked
- Waiter spilt drinks over us
- We argued about something – split up
- Finish with words from question

B

Introduction: importance of food for health. Disagree with statement.

a Parents know what is good for children's health; responsibility to guide them. Need to ensure they have balanced diet (give examples).

b Many children would avoid food with vitamins, minerals, proteins. Fast food, chips, sweets, chocolate: all bad for health, eg sweets cause tooth decay

c Some children might eat all day – become overweight. Others might not eat at all – become too thin.

Conclusion: Restate opinion: need for parents to give guidance.

C

1 Opening: thank for birthday card. Mention 18th birthday meal.

2 Briefly say who was there. Describe what ate – great!

3 One or two paragraphs on what happened:

eg **a** Good things: surprise guest and/or present; sang songs/played games

b Bad things: someone fell ill; family argument

4 Ending: ask about pen friend's 18th birthday.

B Writing

1 When writing your answer you should aim to include various 'ingredients'. Match each writing type **1–3** to the appropriate list of 'ingredients' **a–c**.

1 Informal letter **2** Short story **3** Composition

a
- a clear statement of your opinion
- clear organization and development of ideas
- formal linking words, eg *In addition, However, Therefore*

b
- appropriate opening and closing formulae
- informal language and expressions
- informal linking words, eg *and, but, so*

c
- a variety of past tenses
- a wide range of vocabulary (including phrasal verbs)
- time linkers, eg *as soon as, afterwards, while*

2 Write an answer to one of the questions in Planning above using between **120–180** words. You may follow the relevant plan **(A–C)** or you may write your own. You should aim to include the relevant 'ingredients' from section 1.

For more information on each of the writing types you should look again at the following units.

	Coursebook	Workbook
Composition	3, 8	3, 4, 9
Short story	4, 6	5, 7
Informal letters	1, 9 Ready for writing	1, 2, 10

3 Write an answer to one of the questions below. Choose a different writing type to the one you chose in **2**. Don't forget to make a plan before you start to write.

Timing

In the exam you will have 45 minutes to write each answer. Try following these guidelines when writing your answer to the question below:

5 minutes	Make a plan
35 minutes	Write your answer
5 minutes	Check your work

1 You have recently had a class discussion on the subject of fitness and health. Your teacher has asked you to write a composition giving your opinion on the following statement:

People worry too much about fitness and health.

Write your **composition**.

2 You have decided to enter a short story competition. The competition rules say that the story must begin or end with the words:

My arm hurt so much I felt sure I must have broken it.

Write your **story** for the competition.

3 You recently decided to lead a more healthy lifestyle. Write a letter to your pen friend describing the changes you have made **and** telling him/her what benefits you have noticed so far.

Write your **letter**.

13 Against the odds

Reading

FCE Part 4

Multiple matching

1 You are going to read an article in which people talk about money. For questions **1–15**, choose from the people **A–F**. Some of the people may be chosen more than once. When more than one answer is required, these may be given in any order. There is an example at the beginning **(0)**.

Which person or people

is desperate to have more money?	**0** *E*	
have lost friends?	**1**	**2**
does not want to owe money to anyone?	**3**	
are optimistic about the future?	**4**	**5**
are able to save money for the future?	**6**	**7**
gives in to pressure?	**8**	
inherited some money?	**9**	
say that attitudes to money have changed?	**10**	**11**
mention employment they do not enjoy?	**12**	**13**
have had to change their lifestyle?	**14**	**15**

Money makes the world go round?

Steve Mummery talks to six different people about the importance of money in their lives.

A **Reginald** I don't have a credit card, I've never taken out a loan and I certainly couldn't ask my friends to lend me money. I suppose it's a generational thing. When I was younger you had to get by on what you'd got, watching every penny to make sure you got to the end of the month. It was unheard of in my family to borrow money. Nowadays, people don't think twice before going into debt to buy a new car or whatever. I have to live on the basic state pension, which isn't very much, yet I still manage to put some money to one side each week, just in case I need it later.

B **Ruth** Money's a bit tight at the moment. My husband's out of work and I only work part-time, but we're just about able to make ends meet. Of course, we've had to make a few cuts to adapt to the circumstances. We got rid of the car last month, which has helped enormously, and we've stopped buying new clothes and things. There's no point looking a million dollars if you can't pay the bills. Still, things can only get better and I'm sure we'll sort our situation out, sooner or later.

C **Lester** A year ago I was a hard-up student, struggling to survive on a grant. Then my uncle died and I came into quite a large sum of money. I don't have money to burn but I do have enough to make life more comfortable. Unfortunately, one or two so-called friends of mine thought it gave them the right to depend on me to buy them drinks all the time, and they got quite upset when I refused. I'd rather go drinking on my own than have that type of person around me.

D **Trudy** I've got a job on Saturdays working in a clothes shop. It's really dull, but I get paid quite well, and that gives me the freedom to do things I couldn't afford to if I had to rely on pocket money from my mum and dad. Of course, I spend some of it on going out with my friends, but I've also opened a savings account; I'd like to have a motorbike by the time I'm 18.

E **Bob** I started doing the lottery five years ago, and since then I haven't missed a day. I've only had a couple of small wins, but I feel sure my luck's going to change; the law of averages says it must. I'd do anything to win the jackpot and give up my monotonous job. Any spare money I have is spent on lottery tickets; I've stopped buying records and clothes, and I hardly ever go out now. The fact is, my mates don't bother phoning me up any more, but I don't really mind. I'm prepared to make sacrifices.

F **Alison** Our kids seem to think we're made of money. They always want money for this and money for that; computer games, designer clothes, videos and CDs. I'm not saying we didn't want things when we were kids, but at least we had some idea of the value of things. We'd never have dreamed of asking our parents for the sort of amounts our two, and many others like them, do. I'm sure kids these days think money grows on trees. We've tried saying 'no', but I have to confess we don't always succeed.

2 Find words or phrases in the texts which mean the same as the words given below. The letters in brackets refer to the relevant texts.

1 to save money (A) ______________________
2 we don't have much money (B) ______________________
3 to get by financially (B) ______________________
4 looking very beautiful (B) ______________________
5 having very little money (C) ______________________
6 inherited (C) ______________________
7 have more money than is needed (C) ______________________
8 the biggest prize (E) ______________________
9 we have a lot of money (F) ______________________
10 money is easy to get (F) ______________________

Vocabulary

Wordlist on page 205 of the Coursebook

A Money

1 One of the items of vocabulary in each group is not normally used with the word or words in capital letters. Underline the item which does not fit.

Example:

SPEND	*too much*	*a fortune*	*the receipt*	*£2 on sweets*

You can *spend too much, spend a fortune* and *spend £2 on sweets*, but you cannot *spend the receipt*.

1 PAY	the rent	change	a fine	tax
2 PAY BY	cheque	credit card	debt	direct debit
3 RATE OF	interest	inflation	exchange	bill
4 BUY SOMETHING	on loan	on credit	on impulse	second-hand

5 owe	open	close	credit	**AN ACCOUNT**
6 bank	savings	coin	current	**ACCOUNT**
7 invest	inherit	do	withdraw	**MONEY**
8 sell	repay	apply for	take out	**A LOAN**

2 Complete the spaces with a word or words that you have underlined in **1** above. The first one has been done for you.

1 If it isn't the right size, bring it back to the shop with *the receipt* and we'll change it for you.
2 Could you give me a 10 pence ______________ for the phone?
3 I'm not lending you any more money! You still ______________ me £10 from last week.
4 The paintings by Turner are currently ______________ to the Prado Museum. They'll be back here next month.
5 Have you paid the electricity ______________ yet?
6 **a:** £9.50, please.
b: Here's £10. Keep the ______________ .
7 I hate being in ______________ , which is why I never borrow money from anybody.

B Revision: Lexical phrases

Lexical phrase list on page 124

Complete each of the spaces with the correct form of one of the verbs in the box. You will need to use each verb twice. The first one has been done for you.

get	have	take	come	give	put	make	do

1 He cut himself quite badly, so he was *taken* to hospital, where he was *given* an anti-tetanus injection.
2 He knew he had ________ several silly mistakes in the exam, so it ________ as no surprise to him to hear that he'd failed.
3 Lubowski, a piano teacher for 42 years, ________ great pride in the fact that she had ________ an important influence on the playing styles of some of the world's finest pianists.
4 Recently we've been ________ a lot of difficulty ________ our son to ________ his homework.
5 I had considered ________ research, until I found out just how much time and effort I would need to ________ into it.
6 I've ________ to the conclusion that a lot of these off-piste skiers are just selfish; as well as ________ their own lives at risk, they endanger those of the rescue services who are called out to help them when they ________ into trouble.
7 The director ________ a deep sigh when he saw the figures for June; the company had ________ a loss of £3 million in the first half of the year.

Language focus

Grammar reference on pages 216 and 217 of the Coursebook

A Ability

In five of the following sentences there is a mistake in the part which is underlined. Find the mistakes and rewrite the sentences so that they are correct.

1 <u>I could dance</u> like that when I was your age.

____

2 <u>Trevor could mend</u> the washing machine yesterday; it's working perfectly now.

____

3 <u>I couldn't do</u> the homework last night – it was far too difficult.

____

4 <u>He could hear</u> someone moving about in the kitchen. He went downstairs to investigate.

____

5 I offered to help him but he said <u>he could do</u> it on his own.

____

6 <u>I've never could swim</u> very well.

____

7 I don't understand why he's the manager; <u>he's incapable to organize</u> anything.

____

8 <u>Did you manage to get</u> in touch with Stephen last night?

____

9 Jane's very busy, so <u>she won't can come</u> until later.

____

10 <u>They didn't succeed to get</u> into the final last year; they were beaten 3–1 in the semi-finals.

____

B Phrasal verbs and prepositions

Complete each of the spaces with one of the words from the box. You will need to use some words more than once.

off	on	out	round	up	for	of	from

The trip of a lifetime

In a month's time I'll be setting **(1)** ________ on the trip of a lifetime. My plan is to cycle all the way **(2)** ________ the world, starting and finishing in my home town of Plymouth. It's taken over two years to prepare **(3)** ________ the adventure; planning it, training for it and organizing the finance. I've saved **(4)** ________ about a quarter of the money I need, and I've managed to raise the rest by doing **(5)** ________ my house and selling it **(6)** ________ a lot more than it originally cost me. Fortunately, I've received some sponsorship from a bicycle manufacturer, so I haven't had to pay **(7)** ________ the ten replacement bicycles I've calculated I'll need; I've worked **(8)** ________ that at least five will be damaged in accidents and I'll almost certainly be robbed **(9)** ________ another three or four during the trip.

Understandably, my parents are not very keen **(10)** ________ the idea, and I don't blame them **(11)** ________ wanting to try to discourage me **(12)** ________ going. They still haven't forgiven me **(13)** ________ the worry I caused them when I tried, unsuccessfully, to cycle from Norway to South Africa. They've finally accepted, however, that nothing will prevent me **(14)** ________ attempting it, and my mum has said she'll be the first to congratulate me **(15)** ________ my achievement when I get back in two years' time.

Use of English

FCE Part 1

Multiple choice cloze

Decide which answer **A**, **B**, **C** or **D** best fits each space. There is an example at the beginning **(0)**.

A success story

At 19, Ben Way is **(0)** *already* a millionaire, and one of a growing number of teenagers who have **(1)** ________ their fortune through the Internet. **(2)** ________ makes Ben's story all the more remarkable is that he is dyslexic, and was **(3)** ________ by teachers at his junior school that he would never be able to read or write **(4)** ________ . 'I wanted to prove them **(5)** ________ ,' says Ben, creator and director of Waysearch, a net search engine which can be used to find goods in online shopping malls.

When he was eight, his local authorities **(6)** ________ him with a PC to help with school work. Although he was **(7)** ________ to read the manuals, he had a natural ability with the computer, and **(8)** ________ by his father, he soon began **(9)** ________ people £10 an hour for his knowledge and skills. At the age of 15 he **(10)** ________ up his own computer consultancy, Quad Computer, which he ran from his bedroom, and two years later he left school to **(11)** ________ all his time to business.

'By this time the company had grown and I needed to take on a **(12)** ________ of employees to help me,' says Ben. 'That enabled me to start **(13)** ________ business with bigger companies.' It was his ability to consistently **(14)** ________ difficult challenges that led him to win the Young Entrepreneur of the Year award in the same year that he formed Waysearch, and he has recently signed a deal **(15)** ________ £25 million with a private investment company, which will finance his search engine.

0	**A** yet	**B** just	**C** already	**D** even
1	**A** taken	**B** made	**C** put	**D** done
2	**A** This	**B** That	**C** Something	**D** What
3	**A** said	**B** told	**C** suggested	**D** reported
4	**A** absolutely	**B** totally	**C** properly	**D** thoroughly
5	**A** wrong	**B** false	**C** untrue	**D** unfair
6	**A** provided	**B** gave	**C** offered	**D** got
7	**A** impossible	**B** incapable	**C** disabled	**D** unable
8	**A** promised	**B** invited	**C** encouraged	**D** animated
9	**A** owing	**B** charging	**C** lending	**D** borrowing
10	**A** put	**B** ran	**C** made	**D** set
11	**A** pay	**B** spend	**C** devote	**D** invest
12	**A** couple	**B** few	**C** little	**D** deal
13	**A** having	**B** doing	**C** making	**D** bringing
14	**A** overcome	**B** overlook	**C** overtake	**D** overdo
15	**A** valuable	**B** estimated	**C** priced	**D** worth

FCE Part 5

Word formation

Use the word given in capitals at the end of each line to form a word that fits in the space in the same line. There is an example at the beginning **(0)**.

A narrow escape

Terry Little gave his parents the **(0)** ___*fright*___ of their lives last weekend when he fell nearly 100 metres down one of the **(1)** ____________ cliffs in England. Rescue services were **(2)** ____________ , however, when they found Terry lying unconscious, but alive, on the beach below. 'His condition was **(3)** ____________ good,' said one doctor at Penzance General Hospital, where Terry was taken. His **(4)** ____________ were limited to a few minor cuts and bruises and two **(5)** ____________ teeth. His **(6)** ____________ was described as 'a miracle' by his parents, who had watched in horror and **(7)** ____________ as their son was blown off the cliff by a sudden gust of wind. 'We felt sure he had fallen to his **(8)** ____________ ,' said Terry's father. 'The news that he was safe and **(9)** ____________ well came as an enormous **(10)** ____________ . We certainly won't be going near any more cliffs for a while.'

FRIGHTEN
HIGH
AMAZE
SURPRISE
INJURE
BREAK
SURVIVE
BELIEVE
DIE
REASONABLE
RELIEVE

FCE Part 3

Transformations

Complete the second sentence so that it has a similar meaning to the first sentence, using the word given. **Do not change the word given**. You must use between two and five words, including the word given. There is an example at the beginning **(0)**.

0 We've decided where we're going on holiday.
up
We've ___*made up our minds*___ where we're going on holiday.

1 He telephoned several people before lunch.
calls
He ________________________ before lunch.

2 We found it difficult to choose.
was
It ________________________ for us to make.

3 They can't prove he's guilty.
no
They have ________________________ his guilt.

4 The President offered his congratulations to the players when they won the cup.
congratulated
The President ________________________ the cup.

5 I forgot her birthday last year and she still hasn't forgiven me.
me
She still hasn't forgiven ________________________ last year.

6 The two sides were unable to reach an agreement.
succeed
The two sides ________________________ an agreement.

7 He may be 50, but he can run a marathon in under three hours.
capable
He may be 50, but he ________________________ a marathon in under three hours.

Writing

FCE Part 2

Reports

See pages 152 and 153 in Unit 12 of the Coursebook for more information on writing reports.

1 Read the following Part 2 question.

A group of elderly tourists will be spending a morning in your town as part of a ten-day tour of the region. The local tourist office has asked you to write a report for the group leader, suggesting ways in which the tourists might spend the morning. You should give advice on sightseeing and shopping, as well as information on where they could have lunch.

Write your **report**.

2 The following report was written in answer to the question above. Put the paragraphs in the correct order and write a suitable heading for each one.

Visit to Roxburgh

1

For those who would rather go shopping, the open-air market in the main square is to be recommended for its wide range of goods, all at bargain prices. The square also includes a number of exclusive gift shops, some of which offer generous discounts to senior citizens.

2

Although the group is only in Roxburgh for a short time, everyone is guaranteed a warm welcome and a memorable morning.

3

Some members of the group might like to begin the morning with a visit to the 16th century church, with its impressive and colourful stained glass windows. Within easy walking distance of the church is the Roxburgh Folk Museum, containing numerous exhibits which show what life was like in the town in former centuries.

4

The aim of this report is to give suggestions to a group of elderly tourists on how best to spend their morning in Roxburgh.

5

After a busy morning the visitors can enjoy a reasonably priced lunch in one of several restaurants on the riverfront. Non-vegetarians should try one of the many fresh fish dishes for which Roxburgh is famous.

Find examples in the model of the following:

Different ways of referring to the tourists
eg *Some members of the group*

Different ways of making recommendations
eg *might like to begin the morning with*

Words expressing number or quantity
eg *Some members*

Words and expressions related to cost
eg *all at bargain prices*

3 Writing task

a Read the following writing task.
Some young foreign students are on an exchange programme in your region and are planning to visit your town one day for the afternoon and evening. You have been asked to write a report for the teacher in charge of the group, suggesting ways in which the students might spend their time in your town without having to spend much money. You should give advice on cheap places to go for shopping, entertainment and eating out.

Write your **report**.

Before you write your answer, do the tasks in **b** and **c** below.

b Answer the following questions.
- Who is the target reader of the report?
- Should you write your report in a more formal or informal style?
- What differences do you notice between this task and the one in **1a** above?

c Useful vocabulary
The writing task asks you to give advice on cheap places for the students to go to. Put a tick next to those words or expressions below which suggest that something is **not expensive**.

Words to describe prices

reasonable	exorbitant	inflated	affordable	competitive	PRICES

Words to describe goods

cut-price	overpriced	exclusive	inexpensive	luxury	GOODS

Other words and expressions

good bargains	discounts	special offers
a little on the dear side	good value for money	

4 Now write your report in answer to the task in **3a** above.

Don't forget!

- Divide your report into paragraphs, including a brief introduction and conclusion.
- Give each of your paragraphs a heading.
- You can invent the information in your report if you want to.
- You should not write more than **180** words. Note that each paragraph in the model contains less than 55 words.

14 As pretty as a picture

Reading

FCE Part 3

Gapped text

1 You are going to read an article about a farm animal sanctuary. Eight paragraphs have been removed from the article. Choose from the paragraphs **A–I** the one which fits each space **(1–7)**. There is one extra paragraph which you do not need to use. There is an example at the beginning **(0)**.

Animal Rescue

Katie Smart visits a remarkable woman who dedicates her life to saving farm animals from cruelty.

In 1990 Carole Webb set up a sanctuary to rescue abandoned or mistreated farm animals. She's so dedicated to the well-being of her animals that they've taken over her income, her life and her heart.

0 I

Surrounded by acres of flat land, without so much as a tree in sight, it seems cut off from the rest of humanity. Carole's nearest neighbours are two miles away and she often goes days at a time without speaking to another person.

1 ______

'The animals that arrive here are frightened and in a state of shock,' she explains. 'But they soon change, with love and care. Animals that are often considered stupid show remarkable intelligence once they've got over their fear.'

2 ______

'One day I noticed that one of the lambs had a broken leg. I told the farmer and asked him if he needed any help looking after sick animals. Within a couple of years I'd bought this place and set up my own sanctuary.'

3 ______

'I bottle-fed him, wrapped him up warmly next to the kitchen fire and nursed him back to health.' He is still alive and well, although he's getting a little bad tempered and prefers people not to go near him.'

4 ______

It's hard to believe when you see the size of him that he was found abandoned by the side of a road – cold, weak and hungry. Now he's very much the boss in the sanctuary, and expects to be treated like a VIP, or 'very important pig'.

5 ______

Carole rescued her and three days later Gismo the lamb was born. Then there's Gromit the Friesian cow who was left to die because the farmer couldn't pay his vet's bills, or Petal the goat who suffered terribly for over a year.

6 ______

'The vet refused to let them take her home again. Instead, he gave her to me to take care of. It's amazing she lets anyone go near her after the treatment she received, but she's very happy and loves being with people.'

7 ______

'It was she who came up with the idea of starting up an adoption scheme,' explains Carole. 'Over 400 people have now sponsored an animal, and we have about 40 life members, all of whom have paid money to help keep the sanctuary going.'

A When Carole first moved in, she inherited some 15 sheep from the farmer, including Larry the lamb, whose mother died soon after his birth. 'When I found him he was cold, hungry and close to death,' she recalls.

B Carole openly confesses to preferring the company of animals to humans. 'When I was a little girl I always spent more time with my pets and I could never bear to see any of them suffer.'

C The sanctuary's survival is constantly at risk. It costs Carole £600 a week for hay and animal food, and the vet's bill can be as much as £1,000 a month. 'I remember crying to my friend on the phone, thinking that we'd have to close down.'

D Wiggy the pig, on the other hand, is difficult to get rid of. He's always on the hunt for cakes and biscuits and he won't leave you alone until he's made sure you're not hiding one behind your back.

E Some of the animals arrive in a terrible condition, but at Carole's Farm Animal Sanctuary they all have a future. However, the future is never certain and the sanctuary is beginning to struggle for survival.

F Inspiration for the sanctuary came when Carole, who trained as a veterinary nurse, was living in Hertfordshire. She had a pony, which she kept in a field, and she would often go to the nearby farm to watch the lambs.

G 'She had a broken leg and her owners were supposed to take her back to the vet within a few months so that he could take her plaster cast off. But they didn't return until 15 months later. The poor animal was in agony.'

H In Carole's eyes all her animals have their own personalities, and if they could speak, all would have an alarming story to tell. Take the sheep who was destined for the butcher's, despite her advanced state of pregnancy.

I Carole lives with her 'family' – some 500 sheep, goats, lambs, calves, pigs and chickens – amongst a jumble of old farm buildings. The sanctuary is near Fen Drayton, in a remote area to the west of Cambridge.

2 Find phrasal verbs in the main part of the text which have the following meanings.

1 establish or start (a new organization or business) ____________
2 take control of ____________
3 separate or isolate ____________
4 recover from ____________
5 take care of ____________
6 think of and suggest (an idea) ____________

3 Write the noun form of each of the following words. All the nouns appear in the text.

Adjective	Noun
cruel	____________
pregnant	____________
intelligent	____________
healthy	____________

Verb	Noun
treat	____________
adopt	____________
survive	____________
inspire	____________

Vocabulary

Wordlist on page 205 of the Coursebook

A Crossword: The Arts

Across

1 a person who creates objects out of materials such as wood, stone or metal
4 you go to the theatre to see one
6 Romeo dies in the third ________ of Act V of Shakespeare's play *Romeo and Juliet*.
7 operas are performed in an opera ________
8 a painting showing a view of the countryside
10 you go to an art gallery to see an ________ of paintings

Down

1 the area in a theatre on which the actors perform
2 adjective to describe a painting or other object which is extremely valuable
3 a large group of musicians who play many different instruments together
4 a painting of a person
5 a person who writes music, especially classical music
7 a concert ________ is a place where concerts are given
9 collective noun for actors in 4 across

B Phrasal verbs: Revision

Phrasal verbs with more than one meaning

1 Use the following verbs and particles to make phrasal verbs which have both, or all three meanings, in each group **a–f**.

do	get	take
make	put	fall

out	off	with
up	on	for

Example: _fall_ _for_
fall in love with (someone)
be deceived by (a trick)

a ________________
accept (a challenge/an offer)
start doing (a new sport/hobby)
use or occupy (time or space)

b ________________
postpone (an event)
distract someone
discourage someone

c ________________
fasten or button up (clothes)
repair or redecorate (a room/a building)

d ________________
pretend or claim falsely that something is true
see hear or understand something with difficulty

e ________________
have a good relationship with someone
start or continue doing (work/a job)

f ________________
invent (a story/an excuse)
become friends again (after an argument)

g ________________
accommodate someone (in your house/flat)
increase (prices)

2 Complete each of the spaces with the correct form of one of the phrasal verbs in **1**.

1 I must have put on weight – I can't ____________ these trousers any more.
2 Stop talking everyone and ____________ your work!
3 She decided to get rid of some her books; they were ____________ too much room in her flat.
4 He ____________ that he'd written the poem himself, but we all thought he must have copied it from a book.
5 I wanted to see that opera, but I was ____________ by the cost of the tickets.
6 We often have arguments and fall out, but it's never very long before we kiss and ____________ again.
7 The only way to stop people using their cars is by ____________ the price of petrol.
8 He told me I'd spilt something on my jacket, but I didn't ____________ that old trick. I knew he was after my wallet.

Language focus

Grammar reference on page 217 of the Coursebook

1 Complete the spaces with the correct form of the verb in brackets.

1 I wish we ____________ (have) more time to do the homework. I won't be able to finish it by tomorrow.
2 I wish you ____________ (not/make) so much noise. I'm trying to concentrate.
3 The water in that river looks wonderful. If only I ____________ (bring) my swimming costume.
4 The photocopier's broken down again. I wish I ____________ (know) how to fix it.
5 I wish it ____________ (stop) raining. I want to go to the shops.
6 I'd rather you ____________ (not/tell) anyone about it yet.
7 My wife wants to go to Italy on holiday, but I'd rather ____________ (go) to Spain.
8 It's time I ____________ (buy) some new shoes. These ones have got holes in them.

2 What would you say in each of the following situations? Complete the sentences. The first one has been done for you.

1 Your exams are in two weeks' time and you haven't done any revision yet.
It's high time I *started revising for my exams* .

2 Your classmate hasn't got a watch and is always asking you what time it is.
It's about time you ____ .

3 Your friend wants to come and see you at 8 o'clock, but there's a good film on TV which starts at 7.30.
I'd rather you ____ .

4 You're trying to tell your brother something but he keeps interrupting.
I wish you ____ .

5 Your FCE exam is on Saturday so you won't be able to watch your favourite team play in the cup final.
I wish ____ .

6 Someone stole your video camera on holiday. It wasn't insured.
If only ____ .

7 You have been waiting nearly 30 minutes for your bus to come.
I wish ____ .

8 You have just got back from holiday to find that all your houseplants have died.
If only ____ .

Use of English

FCE Part 5

Word formation

Use the word given in capitals at the end of each line to form a word that fits in the space in the same line. There is an example at the beginning **(0)**.

Modern art

Modern art has become rather **(0)** *fashionable* in the North-East	**FASHION**
of England, and large metallic **(1)** __________ are now fairly	**SCULPT**
commonplace in the region. The **(2)** __________ known of	**WELL**
these is the 200-ton steel figure, Angel of the North, erected in	
Gateshead at the **(3)** __________ cost of £800,000. Many local	**CONSIDER**
people were horrified at the **(4)** __________ to spend such a large	**DECIDE**
sum on a 65-foot metal structure. Nevertheless, the Angel is	
(5) __________ one of the most frequently viewed artworks in	**POSSIBLE**
the world, seen **(6)** __________ by almost 100,000 passing motorists.	**DAY**
A number of **(7)** __________ in Hartlepool were similarly upset	**RESIDE**
when they were greeted one day by the **(8)** __________ of 15	**SEE**
giant, metal balls on a traffic roundabout in the town centre.	
They described the payment of £70,000 for the spheres as	
(9) __________ and felt the money could have been spent on	**RESPONSIBLE**
something more directly **(10)** __________ to the local population.	**BENEFIT**

FCE Part 2

Open cloze

Read the text below and think of the word which best fits each space. Use only **one** word in each space. There is an example at the beginning **(0)**.

Animal mummies

Over the centuries millions of animal mummies **(0)** *have* been discovered in Egypt, **(1)** ________ lying alongside human mummies, and others in their own separate cemeteries. We know, **(2)** ________ course, that the Egyptians mummified pharaohs, queens and priests to ensure **(3)** ________ passage into the afterlife. But why did they bury so **(4)** ________ animals?

Some, **(5)** ________ seems, were pets; in **(6)** ________ same way that possessions were buried **(7)** ________ the use of the dead in the afterlife, a favourite cat, dog or monkey would **(8)** ________ sacrificed in order to keep the deceased company there. Other animals, however, were intended **(9)** ________ gifts to the gods; a crocodile to please Sobek or a cow for Hathor. Whole catacombs were dedicated to particular animals, **(10)** ________ as cats, dogs or birds, **(11)** ________ were buried in large numbers, possibly to mark a religious festival. **(12)** ________ animal was considered too small or insignificant for mummification: snakes, beetles, fish of all sizes and even the eggs of birds and reptiles.

(13) ________ animal mummies were clearly very important to the ancient Egyptians, few studies have been carried out on the subject, perhaps because **(14)** ________ has always been more interest **(15)** ________ human mummies.

FCE Part 4

Error correction

Read the text below and look carefully at each line. Some of the lines are correct, and some have a word which should not be there. If a line is correct, put a tick (✓) at the end of the line. If a line has a word which should not be there, write the word.

Television appearances

0 I must have been on television at about twenty times altogether. Most *at*
00 of the appearances were on daytime chat shows and game shows, but I ✓
1 have also been invited to appear on it a cookery programme, and I made ______
2 a few of comments on a current affairs programme during the last election. ______
3 It all started four years ago, when I was the victim of a mugging me. A ______
4 researcher for a morning chat show phoned and asked to me if I would ______
5 go on the programme and talk about the experience as part of a discussion ______
6 on crime. I didn't get by nervous and I expressed myself quite well, so ______
7 they approached me several times after that, asking me to give my opinions ______
8 on the all sorts of different issues. Some time later I answered an advert ______
9 in a magazine was inviting people to go for an interview for a new game ______
10 show. They asked everyone fifteen general knowledge questions, which I ______
11 had no difficulty answering them, and then we had to talk about ourselves ______
12 for three minutes, to see how we reacted under pressure. Because I had ______
13 been on television before, I felt myself very confident and the next day ______
14 they told me I wish had been accepted. I did really well on that show and ______
15 won £3,000. If only I could win that much every one time I appear on TV! ______

Writing

FCE Paper 2

Read the Paper 2 Writing questions below. Before you write any answers, do the preparation exercises on page 113.

Part 1 You **must** answer this question.

1 Your penfriend's parents have planned a tour of your country and are coming to your area for two days. They are particularly interested in the arts, and your penfriend, Richard, has written to you, asking you for some information which will help them plan their trip.

Read Richard's letter and the notes you have made on it. Then write a letter to Richard, giving him all the necessary information.

> So while I'm in the States visiting my cousins, my mum and dad will be there with you, lucky things! Anyway, they've asked me to find out about the following from you:
>
> • best time to come for arts festivals or any other events
>
> • museums you'd recommend
>
> • anything else which might be of interest
>
> I've told them you're busy during the day, but they'd love to take you out for a meal one evening. Will you have any free time? Let me know as soon as you can – it's only a month before they set off.
>
> All the best
> Richard

Notes:

- Museum of Film and Television & Modern Art Museum (→ museums you'd recommend)
- Sculpture Park (→ anything else which might be of interest)
- Only free on Saturday evening (19th) (→ Will you have any free time?)
- International Dance Festival: 12th - 19th (→ best time to come for arts festivals)
- National Symphony Orchestra: 18th (playing Beatles music!) Interested? Need to get tickets. (→ or any other events)

Write a **letter** of between **120-180** words in an appropriate style. Do not write any addresses.

Part 2 Write an answer to **one** of the questions **2–4** in this part. Write your answer in **120–180** words in an appropriate style.

2 You are studying in England for a year and you see the following advertisement in a local newspaper:

PET SHOP

requires a part-time shop assistant for three months.

Duties include: feeding and caring for pets, serving in shop, advising customers on animal care.

- love and knowledge of animals essential
- previous experience of shop work preferred

Foreign students welcome: must have reasonable level of spoken English

Contact: *Mr P Sayers, Pet Paradise, 38 Portland Road, Hove BN41 6JF*

Write your **letter of application** to Mr Sayers, asking for more information about the working hours and pay.

3 Your town has been given a large sum of money to be spent on **either** a zoo **or** a concert hall. Write a report for the town council describing the benefits to the town of both proposals and say which one you think the money should be spent on.

Write your **report**.

4 You see the following advertisement in a magazine for pet lovers.

Writing Competition

We would like to receive your articles with the following title:

MY SPECIAL FRIEND

Write to us about your pet, telling our readers how it came to be in your family and what makes it so special.

The writer of the best entry will receive a year's supply of food for their pet.

Write your **article** for the writing competition.

Preparation for Part 1

Remember that candidates who write good answers to Part 1 questions attempt to build on the information given by adding relevant points of their own.

In order to prepare for the Part 1 question on page 111, decide first what extra information you could give. Make notes for each of the following:

International Dance Festival:	*What type of dance is performed (eg modern, classical, folk etc)?* *Which countries participate?*
National Symphony Orchestra:	*Cost of tickets?* *Do you think it will be worth going to?*
Museums:	*What type of exhibits are on display?*
Sculpture Park:	*What could you say about the park?* *eg size of park, number of sculptures, your opinion, other things to do there*
Going out for a meal:	*Why are you only free on Saturday evening?*

Don't forget!

You should not write more than **180** words, so you may not be able to include **all** this extra information.

Language preparation

a In **1–8** below complete each of the spaces with one of the phrases from the box.

that struck me	sum up	express an interest
aim of this report	looking forward to	pleased to hear
have no experience of	I like most about her	

1 The ____________________ is to consider the benefits of ...
2 I'm really ____________________ meeting them.
3 Although I ____________________ working in a pet shop, I spent the last two summers helping my uncle in his newsagent's.
4 The first thing ____________________ about her was her lovely smooth fur.
5 I was ____________________ your parents are coming.
6 To ____________________ , I recommend that the money should be spent on the zoo, mainly because ....
7 What ____________________ is her lively nature and almost limitless energy.
8 I am writing to ____________________ in the job I saw advertised in the York Gazette.

b In answer to which question is each sentence written?
eg *Sentence 1, Question 3*

Writing task

Write an answer to the Part 1 question. Then choose one of the Part 2 questions and write an answer.

For more information on each of the writing types you should look again at the following units.

Task type	Coursebook	Workbook
Informal letters	1, 9, Ready for writing	1, 2, 10
Letter of application	5	6
Report	12	13
Article	2, 10	3, 11

15 Mind your language

Reading

FCE Part 1

Multiple matching

1 You are going to read an article about hand gestures. Choose the most suitable summary sentence from the list **A–H** for each part **(1–6)** of the article. There is one extra summary sentence which you do not need to use. There is an example at the beginning **(0)**.

A Gestures help us to remember words.
B The language we speak may influence how much we gesture.
C Words are not always necessary to get the message across.
D The gestures we use may be inherited.
E Gestures can help to reinforce what we say and feel.
F Foreign speakers of English gesture more than native speakers.
G Less physical concepts can be explained with gestures.
H More importance is now given to the role of gestures

Say it with your hands

0	*H*

For many people gestures are an integral part of their speech, and communicating without hand movements of some kind would be difficult, if not impossible. Once considered meaningless and rather distracting, gesticulation is now being taken more seriously as a means of communication, and has been the subject of a great deal of research in recent years.

1	

Politicians have long recognized the importance of gestures and many are taught how to use their hands effectively. Zoologist Desmond Morris has identified at least 11 different gesticulations employed by politicians to add emphasis to their words and convey the strength of their emotions. The thumb and forefinger joined at the tip, for example, accompany the words of a speaker as he or she gives a precise detail or explanation, whereas a hand cutting vigorously and repeatedly through the air helps to make a point very forcefully.

2	

Hands, of course, can also be used to convey meaning more directly and give important information in a conversation. They can even replace speech when demonstrating the size and shape of an object, or showing the direction someone needs to take in order to reach their destination. Early tribesmen used their finger to indicate direction, usually to show other members of the tribe the location of an animal being hunted. Rather like an arrow being aimed at a distant target, the higher the finger was pointed, the further away the animal was.

3	

Recent studies in the US, however, reveal that gestures not only enable us to convey meaning to the listener, but they also aid memory and help speakers find the words they need to express their thoughts and ideas. In one experiment, volunteers were asked to give the word for the following definition: 'an ancient instrument used for calculations'. Those who were allowed to gesture made motions of using the instrument before coming up with the word, 'abacus'; those who were prevented from moving their hands failed to think of the word or took longer to do so.

2 Write the name of the people formed from each of the words on the left. All these people are mentioned in the reading text. There is an example at the beginning **(0)**.

	Person		Person
0 speak	*speaker*	**6** Italy	
1 listen		**7** Jewish	
2 research		**8** immigration	
3 psychology		**9** voluntary	
4 zoology		**10** tribe	
5 politics			

3 Now write the name of the people formed from each of the following words. You will need to use the same endings as those in **2**.

	Person		Person
0 learn	*learner*	**4** participate	
1 electricity		**5** sport	
2 mountain		**6** begin	
3 Finnish		**7** biology	

5

In another study it was found that we tend to gesture more when we try to define words such as 'above' or 'next to', which indicate the position of something, than when defining more abstract ideas, such as 'thought' or 'information'. People who gesture a lot often turn abstract notions into more physical representations: 'comprehension' can be expressed by moving the hands as if you were taking hold of something; 'freedom' can be understood as 'having no frontiers,' an idea which is easier to represent with the hands.

6

Some people gesture more than others, in some cases as much as 40 times more, according to psychologist Robert Krauss of Columbia University in the US. He believes that the speaker's mother tongue has a lot to do with this; the more rhythmic a language, the more gestures its speakers will use. He quotes a study in New York in the 1940s, which found that Italian and Jewish immigrants used their hands more than any groups. The Jews tended to use small gestures whereas the Italians were less restrained.

6

More modern researchers have spent a considerable amount of time investigating gesturing in young people who have been blind from birth. They have discovered that when blind people communicate with each other, they use their hands just as much as sighted people, despite the fact that the speaker knows the listener cannot see his or her gestures. What is more, they use a similar range of gestures to those used by sighted people, suggesting that hand movements are not necessarily learnt by observing others.

4 Write down ten nouns from the reading text which end in *-ion*. If the noun is formed from a verb, write the verb. The first one has been done for you.

Noun	Verb	Noun	Verb
gesticulation	*gesticulate*	________	________
________	________	________	________
________	________	________	________
________	________	________	________
________	________	________	________

Vocabulary

Wordlist on Page 205 of the Coursebook

A Word grid: Education

Use the clues to help you complete the grid with words related to education. When you have all the answers you will find an extra item of vocabulary for number 10 down.

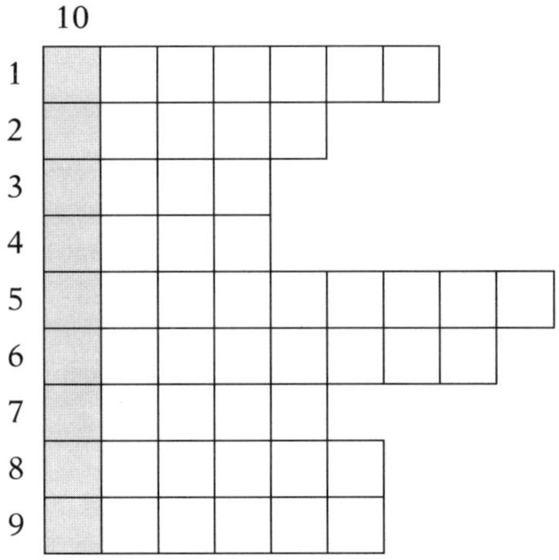

1 children in Britain go to ________ school between the ages of 5 and 11, before they go to secondary school
2 to take an exam again
3 the ________ University offers programmes on the radio and television for students who want to study for a degree at home
4 you can either pass an exam or ________ it
5 an FE college is a college of further ________ for people older than school age
6 maths, history and science are all school ________
7 a ________ school is controlled by the government or local authority. Children do not have to pay to attend
8 ________ and Cambridge are the most famous universities in Britain
9 to study something again in order to prepare for an examination
10 the most senior teacher in a British university department

B Phrasal verbs with *turn*

Phrasal verb list on page 123

Complete each of the spaces with one of the following particles.

off	up	into	on	down	out

1 They offered her the job but she turned it ________ because the salary was so low.
2 I was furious! We arranged to meet at 6 o'clock, but he didn't turn ________ until 7.
3 This building was a dance hall before they turned it ________ a cinema.
4 As soon as he gets up, he turns ________ the television and spends the next three hours watching the cartoons.
5 We got talking, and it turned ________ that we both went to the same school.
6 We've gone too far. We should have turned ________ this road at the last set of traffic lights.

have something repaired
have your ear/nose pierced
have your hair cut/done/dyed
have your head shaved
have your house broken into
have your photo taken
have your tonsils taken out

It's got/it has nothing to do with you.
Can I have it back please?
What has she got on? (= What is she wearing?)

Make (Unit 13)

make a cake
make a complaint
make a cup of tea
make a choice
make a decision
make a film
make a loss
make a mess
make a mistake
make a noise
make a phone call
make a plan
make a profit
make a promise
make a speech
make a will
make an appointment
make an arrangement
make an effort
make an investment
make friends with someone
make fun of someone
make money
make some changes
make sure
make the beds
make up your mind
make yourself at home

Put (Unit 11)

can't/couldn't put my book down
put a lot of time/effort/hard work/energy into (doing) something
put a plaster on a cut (12)
put a record/CD/tape/video on
put one's feet up
put pressure on someone (to do something)
put some money to one side (13)
put someone's arm in plaster (12)
put someone/someone's health/life at risk
put someone in a good mood
put someone in touch with someone else
put someone on a course of antibiotics (12)
put someone up for the night
put the blame on someone for (doing) something

Take (Unit 4)

take a joke
take a long time to do something
take a photo
take a risk
take care of
take courage
take criticism
take interest in
take it or leave it
take my word for it
take notice of
take offence at
take one thing at a time
take part in something (2)
take pity on
take place (2)
take pride in
take someone's advice
take something back to a shop
take some medicine/a pill (12)
take something seriously
take someone's temperature (12)
take someone to a restaurant/out for a meal
take someone to hospital
take someone to school
take the blame for
take the infinitive/gerund
take time off work
take your time
I can't take it any more.
she/he won't take no for an answer

Irregular verb list

Infinitive	Past simple	Past participle
arise	arose	arisen
awake	awoke	awoken
be	was/were	been
bear	bore	borne
beat	beat	beaten
become	became	become
begin	began	begun
bend	bent	bent
bet	bet	bet
bind	bound	bound
bite	bit	bitten
blow	blew	blown
break	broke	broken
breed	bred	bred
bring	brought	brought
build	built	built
burn	burnt/burned	burnt/burned
burst	burst	burst
buy	bought	bought
catch	caught	caught
choose	chose	chosen
come	came	come
cost	cost	cost
creep	crept	crept
cut	cut	cut
deal	dealt	dealt
dig	dug	dug
do	did	done
draw	drew	drawn
dream	dreamt/dreamed	dreamt/dreamed
drink	drank	drunk
drive	drove	driven
eat	ate	eaten
fall	fell	fallen
feed	fed	fed
feel	felt	felt
fight	fought	fought
find	found	found
flee	fled	fled
fly	flew	flown
forbid	forbade	forbidden
forget	forgot	forgotten
forgive	forgave	forgiven
freeze	froze	frozen
get	got	got/gotten (AE)
give	gave	given
go	went	gone
grind	ground	ground
grow	grew	grown
hang	hung	hung

Infinitive	Past simple	Past participle
have	had	had
hear	heard	heard
hide	hid	hidden
hit	hit	hit
hold	held	held
hurt	hurt	hurt
keep	kept	kept
kneel	knelt	knelt
know	knew	known
lay	laid	laid
lead	led	led
lean	leant/leaned	leant/leaned
learn	learnt/learned	learnt/learned
leave	left	left
lend	lent	lent
let	let	let
lie	lay	lain
light	lit	lit
lose	lost	lost
make	made	made
mean	meant	meant
meet	met	met
pay	paid	paid
put	put	put
seek	sought	sought
show	showed	shown
shrink	shrank/shrunk	shrunk
slide	slid	slid
smell	smelt/smelled	smelt/smelled
sow	sowed	sown
speed	sped	sped
spill	spilt/spilled	spilt/spilled
spin	spun	spun
spit	spat	spat
split	split	split
spoil	spoilt/spoiled	spoilt/spoiled
spread	spread	spread
spring	sprang	sprung
sting	stung	stung
stink	stank/stunk	stunk
strike	struck	struck
swear	swore	sworn
sweep	swept	swept
swell	swelled	swollen/swelled
swing	swung	swung
take	took	taken
tread	trod	trodden
weave	wove	woven
weep	wept	wept
wind	wound	wound